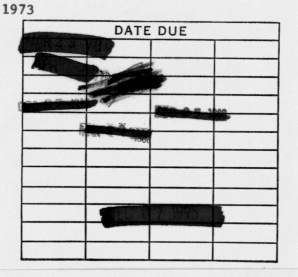

Dostoevsky and Dickens

Dostoevsky and Dickens

A Study of Literary Influence

N. M. Lary

Faculty of Arts, York University, Toronto

Routledge and Kegan Paul

London and Boston

First published 1973
by Routledge & Kegan Paul Ltd
Broadway House, 68–74 Carter Lane,
London EC4V 5EL and
9 Park Street,
Boston, Mass. 02108, U.S.A.
Printed in Great Britain by
The Camelot Press Ltd, London and Southampton
ISBN 0 7100 7554 5
Library of Congress Catalog Card Number: 72-96770

For
Penny, Clarisse,
and Nicky

Contents

Preface

The mark of Dickens is everywhere in Russian fiction. Dostoevsky admires and shares Dickens's ideal of childlike goodness and happiness; life in Biely's St Petersburg is as fragmented and strange as in Dickens's London; Stiva Oblonsky, of all people, in *Anna Karenina* accuses Levin of behaving like a certain Dickensian character who makes light of awkward questions (Steerforth?); Chernyshevsky's heroine in *What is to be Done?* imagines that Dickens's vision of married life is worthy of a born feminist. For Dickens's impact in Russia there were many reasons. He was a realist who saw the new urban society that was emerging and revealed the dreams and ideals that animated it; a psychologist who made his readers look at the unsettled world through the eyes of children; a myth-maker who tried to explain the strange new reality; a humorist who showed that through laughter men still formed a brotherhood; and at times a traditionalist who clung to the simple solutions of an earlier age. Russia in the mid-nineteenth century was caught between two worlds. Serfdom, bureaucracy, and autocratic rule were not acceptable and could not continue as before, yet the rampant individualism and industrial squalor that were developing in the West hardly seemed an alternative. The importance of Dickens for Russians then and later was that he explored the new shape of Western society, at the same time as he looked for a basis for a better and happier life.

Dickens was known and translated in Russia from 1840 on, but his reputation was made in 1847, when the first instalments of *Dombey and Son* appeared in English and, a few months afterwards, in translation. The great age of Russian fiction falls after this date: *Oblomov* came out in 1859, *Fathers and Sons* in 1862, *Crime and Punishment* in 1866, and *War and Peace* in 1868–9. Translations were important in securing Dickens's success both with ordinary readers and with men of letters: one writer who could and did read him in English was Tolstoy, but Gogol, Belinsky, and Dostoevsky were among the many who could not. Even though it is hardly surprising that Gogol's fellow countrymen took to Dickens as much as Gogol himself did when, at the end of his short creative life, he read *Pickwick Papers*, it is interesting to observe how wide and diverse a following Dickens commanded.[1] His works were enlisted in the radical cause of Belinsky and Chernyshevsky, and in the conservative cause of the Slavophiles and nationalists. Tolstoy, the novelist who has most fully revealed man's moral nature, admired his art, as did the symbolist and experimentalist Biely. (Tolstoy's affection survived his conversion; he came to regard most of the world's acknowledged masterpieces as immoral and narrow in class interest, but still he found room in his two categories of 'good art' for the *Christmas Books* and *A Tale of Two Cities* and for *Pickwick Papers* and *David Copperfield*.) Lenin was repelled by the 'bourgeois sentiment' of the English writer – none the less Dickens's position was unshaken by the Russian Revolution. The formalist Shklovsky devoted serious critical attention to him, at a time when in England Jamesian notions of craft and form still offered a reason for deprecating his achievement. Paustovsky and Chukovsky are among the many other writers of the Soviet period who have paid tribute to him.

My interest is in a critical and comparative study of Dickens's influence on Dostoevsky rather than in the general history of Dickens's reputation in Russia. A study of his reputation which did not consider the debt of Russian writers to him could show the universality and richness of his genius. It could also bring out the importance of his position in the literary life of the country (his translators served him well, both through their work and through their connections – one of them, Irinarkh Vvedensky, moved in radical groups, while another, N. A. Beketova, was grandmother of the poet Aleksandr Blok). But until the critical response to Dickens is examined in relation to the tasks and achievements that faced Russian literature, the study of his reputation cannot be a contribution to critical understanding. We need to look at the novels of Dostoevsky, Tolstoy, Biely, and others, to find what Dickens really meant to them and how (and also how well) they used him. The most interesting evidence of an author's reputation

[1] The Russian response to Dickens up to the 1860s is discussed by I. M. Katarsky, *Dikkens v Rossii: Seredina XIX veka* (Moscow, 1966).

◇◆

and influence consists of this kind of non-explicit and sometimes un-conscious indebtedness. I will consider the extent and nature of Dickens's influence on Dostoevsky alone. This is a question I came to as a reader of Dostoevsky concerned to see him in a critical context, but it also confronts the literary historian as part of his task.

Readers of Dickens are faced with this same question. Critics in recent years have often spoken of the Dostoevskian psychology and vision in Dickens's novels in ways which suggest that his influence on Dostoevsky can be taken for granted. But the critics have failed to add much of significance to the evidence that was available to nineteenth-century readers such as Melchior de Vogüé and George Gissing; most of this evidence concerns sentimental and melodramatic characters in immature works (in particular, *The Old Curiosity Shop* and *The Insulted and Injured*). In the light of the apparent scarcity of evidence, Angus Wilson has recently suggested that we should stop looking for any. There is none worth having: 'it is only minor writers who influence you in the sense that you can say, "Yes, that little bit of my book came actually from that writer." . . . Dostoevsky, if he had never read Dickens, would have written in exactly the same way.' The important thing apparently is that the two writers are 'extraordinarily similar' because of their 'extraordinary mixture of black and comic vision which allowed them to see how profound absurdity can be and how utterly ridiculous most of the profound things often are.'[2] But com-parison is interesting only in relation to interpretation, and the critical insight reflected here is inadequate: Dickens and Dostoevsky are reduced to nineteenth-century forerunners of Samuel Beckett; the comparison overlooks the differences in artistic vision which ulti-mately make self-knowledge and the freeing of the imagination so vital for the one, and religious rebirth so crucial for the other. My own view is that there is good (and interesting) evidence of Dickens's influence in Dostoevsky's novels, and further that it is specific enough to indicate what difference Dickens made to them that George Sand, Hugo, Balzac, with admixtures of Paul de Kock and Eugène Sue – who were all read by Dostoevsky – could not have made. Even when the evidence is less than conclusive, the relationship between the two writers is, I think, of critical interest.

For the most part I do not explicitly consider individual contribu-tions to critical problems – to do so would weigh down the text. My

[2] 'Dickens and Dostoevsky', *Dickensian*, September 1970 (supplement).

study is directly relevant to a number of special problems, including such perennial ones in Dostoevsky criticism as the role of Stavrogin and the nature of the ideal embodied in Prince Myshkin. It also bears on an important question which has arisen in modern criticism of Dickens – what view should we take of *Little Dorrit*? If we compare the Dorrit family with the Ivolgins in *The Idiot* we can see that Dickens's powers of imagination do not fully measure up to the portrayal of selfless love; his heroine cannot serve as the touchstone of reality F. R. Leavis finds her to be.[3] My particular concern, however, is with understanding Dostoevsky's achievement. To place Dostoevsky in relation to Dickens is to see him for once in a critical perspective rather than as a philosopher, religious thinker, psychologist, or as a phenomenon entirely *sui generis*. A discipline is imposed on us in our descriptions and in our judgments. We shall see that Dostoevsky usually outdoes Dickens on what is common ground – the perception of suffering, charity, and childlike virtues. On occasion he can even outdo him on Dickens's most characteristic ground – humour. Dostoevsky is truly dramatic – but not for that reason 'better', for what gives the comparisons point is the artistic vision we find in each author. Dostoevsky's vision I deal with directly, and Dickens's chiefly by implication. It so happens that the influence operates in a way which conveniently leads to certain basic questions about Dostoevsky's achievement as a novelist. The influence need not have been of this kind, but it is. And the critical perspective which is thus opened up is particularly interesting.

The cursed questions of existence which Dostoevsky raised owe their urgency and part of their meaning to a society which he knew was threatened with revolution. The awkward dilemma he confronts us with is that in exploring the limits of experience he hopes to find a basis for a stable order, yet too often he undermines not only our complacency but any remaining certainties we have; too much is staked on the venture. In the main Dostoevsky's awareness of the dilemma is reflected in his novels (and, to this extent, offers a measure of his understanding of his society). The structure of his novels, to which I devote special attention, brings this out. The difficulty with him lies in deciding what

[3] F. R. & Q. D. Leavis, *Dickens the Novelist* (London, 1970). This book came out after the main body of my text was complete; none the less, I think the relevance of my discussion is apparent as it stands. Mrs Leavis's chapter on *David Copperfield* makes Dickens's influence on Tolstoy an interesting critical question.

kind of subversive he is: one who is trying to rebuild society from within on a Christian foundation, or a nihilist who would tear everything down because of the impossibility of building an order which adequately reflects the truth. In fact in Dostoevsky's novels we find a remarkable (and ultimately unsuccessful) attempt to understand and master the forces of disintegration. This wish to save and regenerate society was what made Dickens's novels of particular interest to him.

A distinctive reinterpretation of Dickens's achievement does not result from the study I have undertaken here. There are several reasons for this. For one thing, irrespective of influences, we are used to looking at his novels for Dostoevskian insights into the human condition and psyche. For another, there is no sign that Dostoevsky made the discriminations between Dickens's novels which have to be made before we can usefully speak about the artistic vision expressed in them. Influences from the great novels operate side by side with influences from the immature ones (organizing a coherent discussion of so rich and varied an author as Dickens would be difficult in this context). Moreover, in so far as Dostoevsky's view of Dickens can be identified, it is a partial one; he can see individual characters and the theme of brotherhood. He cannot respond to the Dickens who finds in change an outlet for man's sense of purpose and fulfilment (in Dostoevsky change is associated with revolutionary dangers and excitements). The vision that can accommodate change in Dickens's way can also allow for the isolation and sacrifices that go with maturity, and for a rich sense of what life might be. When the ferment in society reaches a Dostoevskian level there is neither time nor need for such perceptions. Although comparisons of this sort will come to mind, I have confined most of my discussion of Dickens within parameters of Dostoevsky's making. The restriction has its compensations; Dostoevsky was no ordinary reader and certainly not a conventional nineteenth-century one.

To generalize is both difficult and necessary. Do Dickens and Dostoevsky complement one another because one writes about change within a basically stable society and the other about a society in the process of disintegration? Or because the sexual passion and religious experience known to Dostoevsky need to be brought into Dickens's world? There is something loose about these juxtapositions. One important reason for reading a novelist is that his concerns are also ours: what is the state of society? how is it changing? what are human needs and happiness? Criticism and comparison are required for intelligent reading. When we look at two novelists from different national literatures, to find what one of them had to learn and could learn from the other, the challenge to our critical faculties is especially great. Part of the difficulty and excitement in reading Dickens and Dostoevsky is that in the end, after their novels have been considered in all their particularity, they confront us with very different visions – one of them sober and ironic and yet a celebration, the other religious, sceptical, and apocalyptic – which do not rest comfortably with one another. Different traditions of thought and different conceptions of human endeavour seem to lie behind them, but we are driven to ask what it is that gives a tradition its strength and direction. Is the tradition that produced Dickens still a vital one, or does a Dostoevskian vision now encompass all?

Acknowledgments

This book first took form as a doctoral thesis submitted at the University of Sussex. My greatest debt is to my supervisor there, Matthew Hodgart, who tried hard to give me a sense of what was worth saying. To the teachers, friends, and colleagues who discussed my work with me at one stage or another I am grateful; I should like to mention in particular Angus Calder, David Daiches, Henry Gifford, Sergei Hackel, Vaughan James, Malcolm Jones, M. M. E. Lainson, Laurence Lerner, John Unrau, and my wife, Diana. I was assisted in my work by grants from King's College, Cambridge, and York University, Toronto.

Acknowledgements

Textual note

For Dostoevsky's literary works, references are to the collected edition, *Sobranie sochinenii*, ed. L. P. Grossman *et al.*, 10 vols (Moscow, 1956–8), and for the letters to *Pis'ma*, ed. A. S. Dolinin, 4 vols (Moscow-Leningrad, 1928–59). The translations are my own, although I have benefited from the attempts of others. For Dickens's novels, references are to the *New Oxford Illustrated Dickens*, 21 vols (1947–58). I have checked the appropriate Russian versions of the novels at all points where my discussion of Dickens's influence hinges on the texts that were available to Dostoevsky.

I

Criminals and angels

'The Bloomsbury that talked about Dostoevsky ignored Dostoevsky's master, Dickens.' If these words of Edmund Wilson's in 'The Two Scrooges'[1] were a challenge, their aim has surely been fulfilled. About a hundred years after Dickens's death not only do we find critical esteem of his work reaching new heights, but his influence on Dostoevsky is widely accepted as fact. And it is felt to be an important fact, confirming that England's greatest entertainer is a serious writer. To be sure, what one author learns from another is not necessarily relevant to what makes them matter to us. The question, on one level of seriousness, is one which the 'novelists haunting the backshop' (once addressed by Henry James in a lecture) are peculiarly suited to tackle. However, if we are given a sufficiently elaborate view of two authors, the claim that one of them influenced the other can lead to a vital tension of critical and descriptive terms as we weigh their works against one another. An example is F. R. Leavis's account of the connection between *Daniel Deronda* and *The Portrait of a Lady*.[2] He brings out the distinctive nature of James's achievement – the attempt to balance American individualism and moral earnestness against the more social civilization of the Europeans, with their manners and cultural baggage – while from a comparison of Isabel Archer and Gwendolyn Harleth he suggests that if George Eliot restricted herself to a specific society, this was in no sense a weakness; her heroine challenges our understanding of what it is to be a responsible moral agent under all the normal workings of social and economic pressure. Because he suspended these conditions, James has less to say about the problem of free choice, although it may appear to lie at the centre of his novel. In this and other ways, the comparison compels us to consider again the terms in which we view each of the novels. A study of an influence can and should be an exercise in understanding.

Is there a meaningful use of critical terms in the many references which are made to Dickens's influence on Dostoevsky? Occasionally yes, but more often they are moves in a literary game of name-dropping. One reason is that too much of the wrong kind of thing is known. The dates of course are right; Dostoevsky, some nine years Dickens's junior, began his literary work at a time when French and Russian translations were spreading Dickens's fame to Russia (and Dostoevsky was dependent on translations, for he read French and some German, but not English). By the time Dostoevsky entered his major creative phase, the bulk of Dickens's work had been completed and was available to Russian readers; the publication of one of several contemporary translations of *Our Mutual Friend* in *Russkii vestnik* in 1864–5 was followed in the same journal by the serialization of *Crime and Punishment*. And there is considerable evidence of Dostoevsky's admiration for the English writer. One report from the Omsk convict prison in the 1850s indicates that he singled out Dickens's novels for attention: 'He would even refuse to read the books brought by the young people, and became interested only twice, in Dickens's *David Copperfield* and *Pickwick Papers*, in the translations by Vvedensky, and took them with him into the hospital, in order to read them.'[3] This in itself suggests that Dostoevsky had brought a special interest in this writer with him to Siberia. In Dresden in 1867, during his honeymoon with his second wife, Anna, he undertook to direct her reading and introduced her to Dickens's novels (possibly in consequence of some little difficulty she had had in selecting books for him from a library). According to the entry in her Diary for 23 May [o.s.] (4 June), Dostoevsky started her out with *Nicholas Nickleby*. This was followed on 27 May by *Marchand d'antiquités*. Three days later they were engaged in a chase for books; Anna notes that in one library 'they had only one of Dickens's novels, and it was out'. But since Anna says nothing more about these novels (whereas she does register her liking for Hugo's *Les Misérables*) it is possible that this was an enthusiasm Dostoevsky failed to impart to her. In any event she stated long after his death in a conversation with the Dosteovsky scholar Leonid Grossman: 'His favourite authors always were Balzac, Walter Scott, Dickens, and George Sand.'[4] A similarly emphatic statement comes from Elena Shtakenshneider, an admirer of his work and, in later years, a friend: 'Dostoevsky's favourite author was Dickens, but he also liked *Gil Blas* and Sue's *Martin l'enfant trouvé*, and more than once told me to read them.'[5] And in the last months of his life, on the day following his greatest public triumph, the speech in which he acclaimed Pushkin as a prophetic and universal genius, Dostoevsky lunched in company with several of his friends and spoke to them in praise of Dickens.[6]

Dostoevsky's own statements are an embarrassment. The specific connections he licenses us to make all relate to Dickens's sentimental and humorous characters. In the *Diary of a Writer* for 1873 he speaks with warm admiration of Little Nell, her grandfather, Oliver Twist, and Pickwick. His wife's *Memoirs* hint that Dickens's comedy was part of their life: 'We bore our relative poverty in a spirit uncomplaining and sometimes even carefree. Fedor Mikhailovich would call himself Mr Micawber and me Mrs Micawber.'[7] Dickens was the author for family reading. Dostoevsky's daughter Liubov' recalls him begging her mother to read Dickens to the children when he was away or too busy. 'During meals, he would question us about our impressions, and evoke episodes from the novels.'[8] He liked miming and acting, and may well have drawn on these talents when he wanted to 'evoke episodes'. He was shrewd enough to see that an uneducated populace would prefer Dumas, with his historical romances, to Dickens: 'I myself often read to soldiers and other people about various Captain Pauls, Captain Pamphiles, and the like. My reading always produced an effect, and this gave me great and even delightful satisfaction. They would stop me to ask for explanations of various historical names, kings, lands and generals. I think that Dickens would have produced much less effect, and Thackeray still less, while the military tales of Skobolev would have produced nothing at all save bored yawns. Oh they are quick people! They can make out the approach straight away. And what humorous, sharp people at the same time.'[9] Needless to say, the difference in response is not disparaging to Dickens. Dostoevsky knew that Dickens was a popular writer, and recognized how effectively he could be read aloud, but knew too the limits of his appeal. And what all this shows is that Dostoevsky knew and enjoyed the Great Entertainer in Dickens.

Dostoevsky enjoyed the Entertainer, but valued him because of the moral influence he could exert, especially on the young. In the last year of his life, he received a letter from a certain Mr Osmidov, who wanted advice on suitable reading matter for his daughter. This gentleman had been keeping her away from all works of literature in order to check her powers of fantasy (perhaps in fear of the example of the pernicious Madame Bovary). Dostoevsky, writing from 'reflection and experience', was driven to protest that this would either choke her fantasy altogether or lead to its excessive and harmful growth. Its development had to be guided. A child particularly needed 'impressions of the *beautiful*'. At the top of Dostoevsky's list of authors came Scott and 'all of Dickens without exception'. He himself had read all of Scott as a boy of twelve, and the influence of this reading had helped him to fight 'tempting, passionate and corrupting impressions'.[10] Possibly Dostoevsky was thinking of the unnatural development of his own powers of fantasy, fostered by Ann Radcliffe and Hoffmann among others. At any rate, Dickens, like Scott, could supply the necessary healthy influence. And in another letter,[11] Dostoevsky indicated that these two writers were among the very first that should be given to children for reading.

The acknowledged influences – some of them suspected by Dostoevsky's earliest readers in England and France – do not take us out of the province of the sentimental and humorous Dickens. There are forced comic characters in the works of Dostoevsky's Siberian period (*The Village of Stepanchikovo* and *The Uncle's Dream*) and, in addition, the Micawberish characteristics of the Marmeladovs; and of course Nellie in *The Insulted and Injured* derives from Little Nell.[12] Because of these influences and because we know that at the time of his later works Dostoevsky continued to admire Dickens, it is easier to accept that his whole art was affected by Dickens than to specify in what way. Such features of Dickens's technique as the dramatic presentation of character, symbolism, and the use of melodrama to show the new conditions of life in cities, are felt to be relevant. But how can this relevance be shown? Of course there is always an easy way with difficulties – to dismiss them, in the manner, say, of George Steiner hoisting a petard: 'The influence of Balzac and Dickens is too obvious and far-reaching to require detailed proof.'[13]

We should be glad that Dostoevsky was not merely idiosyncratic in his tastes, but was he no more than a representative nineteenth-century reader? Here lies the particular importance of Edmund Wilson. He argued that Dickens was a subversive writer and implied that his subversiveness accounted for the attraction he held for Dostoevsky. In support of this view Wilson adduced the murder committed by Jonas Chuzzlewit, which Wilson says probably influenced Dostoevsky. The particular importance of this suggestion presumably stems from this: 'The man of powerful will who finds himself opposed to society must, if he cannot upset it or if his impulse to do so is blocked, feel a compulsion to commit what society regards as one of the capital crimes against itself. With the anti-social heroes of Dostoevsky, this crime is usually murder or rape; with Dickens, it is usually murder.'[14] There is some ambiguity here as to whether Wilson is speaking only about an obsession with murder he has detected in Dickens (in which case it is not obvious that the treatment of murder in his novels reflects a hostility to society) or, additionally, about the motivations of Dickens's criminals (in which case a fair amount of qualification is called for). None the less, let us compare Jonas's crime with a murder committed by a Dostoevskian hero who is undoubtedly a rebel against society: the killing of the old pawnbroker by Raskolnikov in *Crime and Punishment*. Any internal evidence we can find of Dickens's influence in this novel should be particularly convincing, for *Martin Chuzzlewit* is not a book that Dostoevsky is known to have read. The parallels such as they are are not, however, very suggestive. The cramped, secret rooms from which the men emerge are images of their diseased state of mind; they symbolize the alienation of the murderers from society and from themselves. Both men are thought to be in their rooms while they are out committing the deed. They slip back through city streets. Both feel the need for companionship after the crime. And both suffer from guilt but not remorse.

The problem, given the parallels, is one of what we can say. That Dickens inspired Dostoevsky to write about crime? – think of the host of murderers in the works of Ann Radcliffe, Hoffmann, and Poe, to name but a few. That Dickens had something to teach about the psychology of guilt? – questions of guilt and repentance exercised Dostoevsky's mind quite independently; he had stood trial for conspiracy and faced a firing squad, and had lived among criminals and revolutionaries. Or could we say that Dickens showed that the murder was a natural consequence of an intolerable society? – or that he identified with the murderer in a particularly significant way? Philip Collins[15] is surely right in suggesting that Dickens was drawn to the subject chiefly out of a liking for excitement; and he indicates the proper scale of Jonas's interest in characterizing him as a 'vicious and terrified little man'; Jonas is driven by greed in his attempt to murder his father, and in the killing of Tigg Montague by fear of blackmail. Perhaps it could be claimed that each of the crimes is characteristic of the society in which it occurs. In *Martin Chuzzlewit* (also in *Oliver Twist*) we see men destroying themselves under the impulsion of the basic law of political economy – self-interest. Likewise Raskolnikov lives in a world in which this law has superseded every other and personal charity no longer has a place. His own motives are more complicated (and as we know closer to Rastignac's in *Père Goriot* than to those of any character in Dickens); he wants to prove himself a great man, and dreams of becoming a benefactor to mankind. Utilitarian considerations enter into his assessment of the crime, and hence in looking for an influence it might be more profitable to look to *Hard Times*, with its attacks not only on the principle of self-interest, but on the utilitarian calculus and the tendency to reduce questions of behaviour to statistics. After all, Jonas is little more than an exhibit in a rogue's gallery. In *Hard Times* as in *Crime and Punishment*, we find a sister who wishes to sacrifice herself for the sake of a beloved brother and to marry a new-made man who spouts the economic slogans of the new age; and both brothers commit a crime which is somehow implicit in the new prevailing ideology.

Further parallels could be touched on. But surely they will have an air of irrelevancy beside the questions we most need to discuss after reading Dostoevsky's novel. The ideological questions cannot really be considered in abstraction from the particular situation of the Russian intelligentsia, who were cut off from the people and from a national tradition. The radicals among them, led by Pisarev and Chernyshevsky, subscribed to a strange mixture of utilitarianism and socialism; it is this which was the specific object of Dostoevsky's attack, as Joseph Frank has shown.[16] And the more general significance of the book must take us into questions of psychology and religion. Nowhere else in Dostoevsky's work is contradiction so deeply written into the nature of the world, and action so utterly unable to achieve its intention. Raskolnikov is imprisoned by his mother's love, and the sacrifice his sister wants to make for his sake is in fact an impossible burden for him to accept. Marmeladov marries a widow to rescue her from starvation, and drags her and her children still deeper into misery; she accepts him, yet reproaches him for not living up to the expectations fostered in her 'almost aristocratic' youth. The police-examiner Porfiry wants to save Raskolnikov, but behaves like a torturer. The only escape for many of the characters lies in madness. The murder itself is a mad act (or as R. D. Laing has suggested, a not invalid response to a mad situation).[17] Raskolnikov is in effect killing himself by making it impossible to be his warm, outgoing self; the crime is necessary for him to perceive the truth about his nature. Suffering seems as much a metaphysical and moral necessity as an economic one. As Dostoevsky wrote in a review of *Anna Karenina*: 'It is so clear and understandable as to be obvious that evil is concealed in mankind deeper than the physician-socialists suppose; that in no organization of society will evil be avoided; that the soul of man will remain the same; that abnormality and sin come from it; and that, finally, the laws of man's soul are so unknown to science, so uncertain and so mysterious, that there are and can be no physicians nor even *final* judges save He Who says "Vengeance is mine; I will repay".'[18] In *Crime and Punishment* it is as if Dostoevsky were showing that man's salvation or spiritual resurrection can come about only when he recognizes the necessity of evil.

The issues raised by *Crime and Punishment* go far beyond anything arising from Jonas Chuzzlewit and his actions. Yet I think that Wilson was correct in suggesting that Dostoevsky was influenced by this character, and that we can look to *The Eternal Husband* (1870) in order to see this. The hero, Velchaninov, is troubled by memories of the past and has been suffering from a bad conscience. A strange figure with black crape on his hat begins to follow him about and wait beneath his windows. One night Velchaninov is disturbed by a nightmare: a crowd of people in a room are accusing him of some crime, and the key to his guilt or innocence lies with someone whose face he once knew, and who refuses to speak. In a fit of rage, Velchaninov begins striking him when, all at once, everyone cries out and turns towards the door, and Velchaninov awakens to the ringing of the door-bell. He goes to the door of his flat and finds no one there. He begins to fear he is losing the ability to distinguish between fantasy and reality when the man with the crape turns up – another figment of his mind, he thinks at first, but then he recognizes Trusotsky, the husband of a former mistress of his. By chance this man found out about the affair after his wife's death, and for reasons he does not understand he has been driven to seek out her lover. He acts the part of old friend, yet teases Velchaninov's curiosity and engages in strange buffoonery, without revealing the full extent of his knowledge. One night when Trusotsky is staying in the flat, Velchaninov wakes up in the dark, sensing that someone is standing in the room. Terrified, he calls out.

For five minutes there is complete silence, then at last barely two feet away, he hears Trusotsky's voice asking for 'a very necessary household object' (presumably a chamber-pot). On another occasion Velchaninov falls asleep after a fit of illness, tended by his awkward friend, and the nightmare he has had once before recurs. The strange figure in the dream turns out to be Trusotsky; the crowd of people rush to the door and another crowd force their way in, carrying something, when again the bell rings. Instinctively Velchaninov reaches out and awakens to find a man stretched over him, holding a blade. There follows a fierce struggle in the dark, and eventually he overpowers his assailant, Trusotsky.[19]

This outline cannot convey the way in which Dostoevsky brings out Trusotsky's ridiculous nature and at the same time the ugliness of Velchaninov's treatment of him; and it leaves out of account the marvellous comic twist by which the underlying justice is reasserted in their original relations as between cuckold and paramour, while the latter is allowed to expiate his original guilt and the former his attempt at murder. But consider certain similarities in *Martin Chuzzlewit*. During Montague's and Jonas's trip into the country, groups of people stare at them from almost every house. Montague is fearful of Jonas; in a flash of lightning he sees or thinks he sees Jonas aiming a bottle at his head. After an accident and another murderous attempt by Jonas, they reach an inn. Montague double-locks his door for safety, but in the room there is another door locked on the outside. The thought of this door fills his dreams. There is some dreadful secret connected with it for which he is responsible, but at the same time it conceals some 'terrible creature', an enemy of his. To his horror the creature's name is whispered to him, and he awakens to find Jonas standing beside his bed watching him. Jonas, it appears, has come in through the mysterious door, and claims, by way of excuse, that he was simply looking for a bellrope.[20]

The similarities are, I think, telling ones. And in view of these parallels, we might suspect a minor influence in *Crime and Punishment* as well. But will any of this show more than that Dostoevsky responded to and used the melodramatic element in Dickens? This was an area of similarity Dostoevsky's first English readers, Gissing among them, had noted. In suggesting that the two authors shared a subversive view of society, Wilson was dressing up some old knowledge in a new disguise. If to the fact that Dostoevsky admired the sentimental and comic pages in Dickens, we have simply added the claim that he was gripped by the spine-chilling ones as well, we are still left with Dostoevsky as a very complete nineteenth-century reader of Dickens. Of course, the Russian writer is the more complicated of the two. Perhaps then we should say that Dostoevsky valued Dickens's ideal and villainous characters while recognizing that human psychology was a bit more intricate? To anyone who looks at what Dostoevsky makes of Little Nell in *The Insulted and Injured,* this would seem an obvious suggestion to make. And certain remarks of his lend weight to this approach. In *The Eternal Husband* (ch. 4), he describes the 'family readings' held by the Trusotskys together with Velchaninov in a quiet provincial town: 'Velchaninov would read and Trusotsky too would read; to Velchaninov's surprise, he read aloud very well. Natalia Vasilievna would be sewing and would always listen quietly and steadily to the reading. They read novels by Dickens, something from the Russian journals, and sometimes something "serious".' The significance of Dickens here, of course, is that he is the great celebrator of family life, and Velchaninov, the family friend, is in fact the lover of Trusotsky's wife, Natalia. The dubious role of the ideal is further indicated in the notebooks[21] for *The Raw Youth*: 'New people are going about, all of them bearded; but try walking down a street with the idea of telling from [a man's] physiognomy: has he read Pickwick Club?' In the same notebooks the ambitious young hero of Dostoevsky's first-person narrative expresses his revulsion for Dickens's moving pictures of childhood: 'If Touchard is described, then immediately after Touchard a curse on authors describing childhood (Copperfield). And then that . . . I would flog those orphans.' The vehemence of these words suggests that this character is still vulnerable to pity, although as a man of the new age he might hardly bring himself to admit it.

We could say that Dostoevsky admired Dickens's characters but that in putting them to his own uses he treated them with greater psychological and social realism. I think, however, the question is a more interesting one. Wilson was right to suggest a subversive Dickens influenced a subversive Dostoevsky – but the connection cannot be made in the way he thought. To show how it can be made is the subject-matter of this book. At the same time, the 'subversive' influence will have to be reconciled with Dostoevsky's liking for the sentimental characters. He valued them because they could be a formative influence on the young but he did not regard Dickens as a childish writer. Elena Shtakenshneider[22] once started to discuss this with him:

> One day I came to the Dostoevskys' and met him in the very first room. 'Yesterday', he said, 'I had an epileptic fit, my head is aching, and on top of everything that fool, Averkiev, has made me angry. He was running Dickens down and saying that he wrote *trifles* (*bezdeliushki*), children's tales. How could he understand Dickens! He cannot even conceive the beauty of him and has the nerve to speak. I wanted to say Fool to him, and I think I did say it, only you know in rather a subtle way. I was embarrassed because he was my guest and I was in my own home, and I was sorry I was not, say, at your place, where I would have called him a fool outright.'

(Anna came into the room at this point and the conversation was not pursued.) Dostoevsky's admiration for the 'good' characters – and most of his statements come from the later part of his life – will have to be reconciled not only with the influence of the 'bad' ones, but with his own mature interests as a reader and a writer.

There are certain other problems. We know that Dostoevsky read *Pickwick Papers*, *The Old Curiosity Shop*, *Oliver Twist*, and *David Copperfield*. He had French editions of *Dombey* and *Bleak House* in the library he assembled in the last years of his life (in the authorized translations of 1869 and 1871 respectively).[23] He must have known *Nicholas Nickleby* since he gave it to his wife. Beyond that, we have his recommendation that Osmidov's daughter should read 'all of Dickens without exception'. This recommendation, taken on its own, might simply signify his willingness to vouch for any novel written by Dickens. Taken in conjunction with a statement from the second of the articles he wrote on the death of George Sand, that Dickens had humble characters of a certain kind in 'almost every novel' (*Diary of a Writer*, June 1876), it should encourage us to draw on all of Dickens's novels in a search for influences. Of course, caution is needed. And there is the question of when Dostoevsky is likely to have read any given novel by Dickens.

One further difficulty arises – the one we started out with – that of using critical terms meaningfully, so that necessary distinctions shall be preserved. This can be briefly illustrated by a comparison of Jonas Chuzzlewit's suicide with Kirillov's in *The Devils*. The descriptions of Chevy Slyme cracking and eating nuts and of Verkhovensky devouring a chicken, of each of them waiting outside the door, and then going in and finding the victim standing in an angle of the wall – all point to an influence, although whether or not there was one is not immediately to the point. Kirillov's final cry of 'now, now, now, now . . .', repeated ten times over, is like Jonas's 'I've not had time. I have not been able to do it. I – five minutes more – two minutes more! – only one!' In Jonas's words there is despair and an imitation of time moving to its final cessation; in Kirillov's – a resolve to make time stop, and despair of succeeding. But Kirillov's words are truly dramatic, because from the start he has been obsessed with the notions of time and suicide. Their dramatic import appears yet more clearly in the original, for the Russian *seichas* means not only 'now' but 'at once' and (literally) 'this hour'. This is not to say that Kirillov's death brings us into the domain of tragedy, as George Steiner seems to think when he compares Kirillov's cry with Lear's 'never, never, never, never, never'.[24] In registering the finality of death and the fearfulness of the destructive forces that have been unleashed, Lear is evoking something much more general than Kirillov. If a choice had to be made, it would be preferable to describe Kirillov's death as melodramatic rather than tragic, although it must be possible to describe similarities without obliterating distinctions and to use critical terms without losing an awareness of their limitations. To use critical terms meaningfully involves having critical interests. In the absence of critical interests a study of influences is sterile. Accordingly in what follows I will concentrate on a new understanding of Dostoevsky's achievement as a novelist and on books in relation to which I find the influence most interesting.

Notes

1 *The Wound and the Bow* (Cambridge, Mass., 1941), p. 1.
2 In *The Great Tradition* (London, 1948).
3 P. K. Mart'ianov, *Dela i liudi veka*. Quoted in *F. M. Dostoevsky v vospominaniiakh sovremennikov*, ed. A. S. Dolinin (Moscow, 1964), vol. I, p. 240.
4 *Dnevnik 1867 g.* (Moscow, 1923), pp. 45–6, 100, 107, 113; L. Grossman, 'Bal'zak i Dostoevsky', *Tvorchestvo Dostoevskogo* (Moscow, 1928), p. 73.
5 *Dnevnik i zapiski* (Moscow-Leningrad, 1934), p. 462.
6 L. Grossman, *Zhizn' i trudy F. M. Dostoevskogo: Biografiia v datakh i dokumentakh* (Moscow-Leningrad, 1935), p. 303.
7 *Vospominaniia* (Moscow-Leningrad, 1925), p. 127.

8 *Fyodor Dostoyevsky* (London, 1921), p. 203.
9 'Knizhnost' i gramotnost', II', *Stat'i*, p. 143.
10 Letter no. 766, *Pis'ma*, vol. 4, p. 196.
11 No. 789, *Pis'ma*, vol. 4, p. 222.
12 See M. H. Futrell, 'Dostoyevsky and Dickens', in *English Miscellany*, ed. Mario Praz, 7 (1956); I. M. Katarsky, *Dikkens v Rossii* (Moscow, 1966); B. G. Reizov, 'K voprosu o vliianii Dikkensa na Dostoevskogo', *Iazyk i literatura*, 5 (1930).
13 *Tolstoy or Dostoevsky* (London, 1960), p. 197.
14 *The Wound and the Bow*, pp. 16, 98f.
15 *Dickens and Crime*, 2nd edn. (London, 1964), p. 279.
16 'The World of Raskolnikov', *Encounter*, 26, June 1966.
17 *The Self and Others* (London, 1961), pp. 50ff., 162ff.
18 *Diary of a Writer*, July–August 1877, ch. 2, iii.
19 *The Eternal Husband*, ch. 2, pp. 447f., ch. 9, pp. 505f., ch. 15, pp. 560f. (in *Sobranie sochinenii*, vol. 4).
20 *Martin Chuzzlewit*, ch. 42, pp. 644, 646, 652f.
21 In *Literaturnoe nasledstvo*, vol 77 (Moscow, 1965), pp. 256, 296.
22 *Dnevnik i zapiski*, pp. 462ff.
23 L. Grossman, ed., *Seminarii po Dostoevskomu* (Moscow, 1922), p. 32.
24 *Tolstoy or Dostoevsky*, pp. 211ff.

2

The community of the humble

All his life Dostoevsky was a passionate reader. Shakespeare, Schiller, Corneille, Racine, Balzac, Hoffmann, and Pushkin, among others, captured his imagination from an early date, and he spoke of them with enthusiasm in the letters he wrote when he was a student at the Military Engineering Academy in St Petersburg in the 1840s. Schiller, in particular, transported him into a world of exalted passion. 'I have crammed Schiller, spoken Schiller, raved Schiller . . . the name of Schiller has become part of myself, a sort of enchanted sound, calling forth so many dreams' (1 January 1840). Books were more than an escape; they were a means to the discovery of reality. 'To learn what man and life mean – I am making fair progress in this; I can study characters in the writers with whom the best part of my life is freely and happily spent; about myself I'll say nothing more. I have faith in myself. Man is a mystery. It has to be puzzled out, and if you spend all your life puzzling it out, do not say it was a waste of time. I am busying myself with this mystery because I want to be a man' (16 August 1839). In September 1844 he stated: 'To study the life of people is my principal aim and enjoyment, so that, for instance, I am now convinced of the existence of Famusov, Chichikov, and Falstaff.' At the same time reading stimulated his creative imagination, supplied him with subjects, helped him to discover that he should be a novelist rather than a dramatist. During his work on *Poor Folk* he said in a somewhat elliptic note (24 March 1845):[1]

when I am not writing, I read. I read an awful lot, and reading acts on me strangely. Something which I read and reread long ago, I'll read again, and it's as if I was tensing myself with new forces; I get into everything, understand it clearly and draw from it the ability to create.

As for writing drama – well brother, for that, years of labour and

tranquillity are needed, for me at any rate. Now is a good time
for writing. Drama has fallen into melodrama. Shakespeare grows
pale in the twilight and through the mist of [our] playwrights,
seems a god, like the appearance of a spirit on the Brocken or the
Harz. But perhaps in summer I'll write. Two or three years and
we shall see, but for now we'll wait!
Brother, in relation to Literature, I am not the man I was two
years ago. Then it was child's play, nonsense. Two years of study
have given me a lot and taken a lot away.

As during his work on *Poor Folk*, so afterwards books supplied his
imagination with materials to work on. Sometimes it took years before
the stimulus given to him by his reading could find an outlet in his
own writing, but Dostoevsky had a long memory for the books he
loved. Liubov' asserts that her father, 'who forgot his wife's name and
the face of his mistress, could remember all the English names of the
characters of Dickens and Scott which had fired his youthful imagination, and spoke of them as if they were his intimate friends'.[2] Her
biography is notoriously unreliable as a source, so it would be dangerous to lay much stress on her suggestion that Dickens had inspired
her father's 'youthful imagination'. But as to Dostoevsky's memory
for books other than his own, there is evidence enough.

His imagination worked through the interaction of newspaper facts,
real scenes and events, social questions, conscious and unconscious
literary memories, hallucinations, psychological analysis, and (in the
later novels) ideology. A journalistic piece he wrote in 1861, 'Petersburg Visions in Verse and Prose',[3] shows the way in which it operated.
His starting point in this particular instance was an article he had read
in the papers about a retired petty official, a certain Soloviev, who had
died in poverty and deprivation, leaving 169,022 roubles in silver
among his papers. Dostoevsky relates the facts about this miser, but
even as he describes them literary analogies with Gogol and Molière
suggest themselves: Soloviev was a 'new Pliushkin' or a 'new Harpagon', dying in terrible poverty, on top of heaps of gold. The subject
changes to a description of the streets of St Petersburg (it appears that
Dostoevsky has been describing some reflections he was having as he
was out walking), when suddenly he speaks of a figure 'not real but
fantastic' flitting before him in the crowd. The apparition had the
vividness of a hallucination:

a lopsided hat with a broken rim wandered on the crown of his
head. Tufts of grey hair were bursting out underneath it and fell
on the collar of his cloak. A doorkeeper, scraping snow from the
pavement, deliberately tossed a whole shovelful onto his feet;
but the old man didn't even notice it. As he drew even with me,
he glanced at me and winked an eye, a lifeless eye, as though it
was a deadman's eyelid being lifted before me, and at once
I realized that this was the same Harpagon who had died with
half a million on top of his rags. . . .

As Dostoevsky starts to probe into his psychology, he turns into a
'colossal figure': a deliberate recluse, indifferent to the scenes of luxury
in the city streets, content to enjoy his sense of power without needing
to exert it. But now Dostoevsky feels he is plagiarizing Pushkin's
Miserly Knight, and, so, must have gone wrong. He makes a fresh
start: 'No doubt somewhere sixty years ago, Soloviev was an employee,
he was young, youthful, about twenty . . .', and Dostoevsky begins a
new story. Even now, however, he suddenly switches from the name
Soloviev to Akaky Akakievich, as if to indicate that the slow, careful
saving forced on the hero of 'The Cloak', who was a symbol of the
ordinary man in St Petersburg, could turn into a passion for miserliness.

This account is invaluable. It shows how freely images associated
and interplayed in Dostoevsky's mind, and the multiplicity of influences to which he was open; warns that it is dangerous to overstress
the importance of any particular one; suggests that he himself was
sometimes unaware or only half aware of the sources of his inspiration.
Soloviev never found fictional embodiment, but those characters
which did passed through the same formative process. Dostoevsky's
description of it is an encouragement to look for influences in his
novels. If we can find what they had to contribute to Dostoevsky's
creation, they may help us to grasp what the distinctive nature of his
writing is. For the later fiction, his letters and in particular his notebooks
offer a partial record of the genesis of his characters, but the final stage
of their history is the novels themselves. This, of course, is the most
important stage, since it is in relation to their works that a study of the
relationship between two authors becomes an interesting critical
question. The genetic material must be consulted where it is relevant,
but for Dostoevsky's early work it is, for the most part, lacking.

Were Dostoevsky's beginnings as a writer influenced by Dickens?

The evidence relating to his knowledge and opinion of Dickens at this period is very inadequate. It is beyond reasonable doubt that before he left for Siberia he knew at any rate one or two of Dickens's novels. While the letters that have survived from this period contain no mention of Dickens, there is a reference in the 'Petersburg Feuilleton' of April 1847,[4] in which he speaks of a short story, now forgotten, that had particularly impressed him. It was, as he saw it, a story from everyday life: a woman in poor health; her husband, not ill-intentioned but unaware of her needs and feelings; and an only daughter. One evening some of the daughter's friends had come to play, and in the course of their mad games they broke a mirror. The upshot was that when the husband came home drunk he attacked his wife furiously. 'Three days later she was in bed, and in a month she died of consumption. What, because of a broken mirror? Is that possible? Yes. In any case she died. A sort of Dickensian charm is diffused in the description of the last minutes of this quiet, unknown life!' *Dombey* did not begin to appear in Russian translation until the summer of 1847, some nine or ten months after the first English instalment, so it is hardly likely Dostoevsky had in mind the death of Mrs Dombey or of Paul, but those other victims of society's cruelty, Little Nell and Smike, are possibilities.

Statements made in later years confirm that he knew Dickens's work at this early date. In 1870 he wrote to N. N. Strakhov:[5]

> Who is this young professor who with his leaders in *Golos* has 'utterly slaughtered Katkov, so that he isn't even read anymore'? The name of the happy man! Write to me quickly, for God's sake, enlighten me! Long since, some twenty years ago, when *Vanity Fair* first came out in England, I called on Kraevsky, and to my words that maybe Dickens would write something and that it could be translated for the New Year, he suddenly answered: 'Who? Dickens? Dickens is slaughtered! Now Thackeray has appeared there and slaughtered him outright. No one even reads Dickens now!'

The likely date of this episode is sometime before the autumn of 1847. Obviously it has to be after January 1847, when the first monthly part of *Vanity Fair* came out; and it could hardly be after September 1847, when Kraevsky's own journal, *Otechestvennye zapiski*, began to publish a translation of *Dombey* and when, thanks in particular to Vvdensky's translation in *Sovremennik*, Russian readers were beginning to recognize Dickens as the major European writer of the age. Dostoevsky's proposition is not quite as interesting as it might at first seem. In the first place, he could well have been thinking of a Christmas Tale rather than a full-scale novel (the talk of translating something for the New Year rather suggests this). In the second, because of the impersonal construction (*i k novomy godu mozhno budet perevesti*) it is not at all certain he was interested in doing the translation himself. After the enormous critical success of *Poor Folk*, Dostoevsky regarded himself as a novelist in his own right. He was full of projects, and busy writing *The Landlady* and *Netochka Nezvanova*. It seems unlikely he would have wanted to interrupt his own work, in order to engage in something which – however great his admiration for Dickens – would have been a form of literary hackwork (and his own commitments to Kraevsky would hardly have allowed him to do so). It seems the less likely, as any translation by him would have had to be at second hand, by way of a French or German version (not in itself an uncommon practice). What is possible is that Dostoevsky approached Kraevsky with a view to obtaining some translations for his brother, Michael, as he had indicated he would do in a letter of April 1847 (no. 45, *Pis'ma*, vol. 1). Nevertheless, Dostoevsky would hardly have made the offer if he himself had not been particularly interested in Dickens. Before beginning his own work, he had thought of translating Eugène Sue's *Mathilde*; he did, in fact, translate Balzac's *Eugénie Grandet*; and he started on George Sand's *La dernière Aldini*. At the same time, and later too, he put considerable effort on behalf of his brother, who was to do the translations, into an attempt to bring out an edition of Schiller's works. As all of these authors were particular favourites of his, it would seem likely Dickens was too.

So far, however, the evidence goes back no further than the first part of 1847. Dostoevsky's references to Dickens in the two articles he wrote in the *Diary of a Writer* (1876) upon the death of George Sand may point to an earlier date, and a deeper knowledge. He recalls the enthusiasm with which he first read George Sand, and attempts to indicate her place in the intellectual life of the time, speaking throughout less as a cultural historian than as a representative of the generation of the Forties, alive to the ideas about him:[6]

> She first came out in Russian sometime in the mid-Thirties; unfortunately, I don't remember which was the first of her

works to be translated, nor when, but the impression she produced is surely the more remarkable. I think that everyone was struck just as I was, then still a youth, by the chaste, supreme purity of her types and ideals, and by the modest charm of the austere, restrained tone of her narrative – and such a woman was going about in trousers and given to debauchery!

He mentions the feverish excitement with which he first read her, at the age of sixteen, that is to say in 1837–8, and continues:

I think I am right in saying that George Sand, at any rate in my recollections, at once took virtually first place, here in Russia, among that whole pleiad of new writers who were suddenly celebrated and trumpeted throughout Europe. Even Dickens, who appeared here almost at the same time as she, came second, maybe [as though here Dostoevsky were weighing his memories against each other and against his later opinions], in the consideration of our public.

Confirmation that Dostoevsky was aware, at the time, of Dickens's importance is provided by *The Devils* (1871–2), in which the men of the Forties were satirized in the person of old Verkhovensky, who had published the results of his researches into 'the extraordinary nobility of character of some kind of knights at some kind of epoch or something of the sort' in a 'progressive journal which translated Dickens and preached George Sand'.

In the early and mid-Forties, Dostoevsky was fairly 'progressive' himself, sufficiently so to find his friends among Belinsky and his group after that critic's enthusiastic acclaim of *Poor Folk* in 1845. Because of the way Dostoevsky subsequently links the names of George Sand and Dickens (who in the two articles on the French writer is mentioned three times), it is tempting to speculate that the young Dostoevsky not only read Dickens, but saw him as a man who, like George Sand, was reviving faith in the ideals of 'liberty, equality and fraternity', and giving them new meaning. Dostoevsky recalls the prevailing disillusionment with the French Revolution – which had led only to new despotism and the triumph of the bourgeoisie – at a time when 'even science (the economists) turned – with brilliant spokesmen, who came as if with a new word – to mock and condemn the utopian meaning of those three words for which so much blood had been shed'. But this mood of cynicism was to be shattered: 'new men appeared, and boldly proclaimed that it had been needless and wrong to interrupt the cause; that nothing had been achieved by a political change of conquerors; that the cause had to be pursued; that the renewal of man had to be a radical, social one'. In the articles he does not attempt to define his former attitude to the 'new men' – Saint-Simon, Fourier, Lamennais, Cabet – who were discussed in the Petrashevsky circle, which Dostoevsky attended from 1847 until his arrest in 1849 on a charge of revolutionary conspiracy. Instead he confines himself to George Sand, whose historical importance was that, through her novels, the ideas of the Utopian Socialists reached a large public in Russia. For his part, Dostoevsky speaks at some length about the moral purity of her heroines, which, he repeats, struck him from the beginning; and he goes on to say that George Sand's 'radical social' transformation of mankind really amounted to the Christian ideal. 'She based her socialism, her convictions, hopes and ideals on the moral feeling of man, on the spiritual thirst of mankind, on its striving towards perfection and purity, and not on ant-[heap] necessity. She believed unconditionally in the human personality . . . , heightened and extended her conception of it all her life, in each of her works, and thus her thought and feeling coincided with one of the basic ideas of Christianity.' Now this could simply be Dostoevsky's view from the retrospect of 1876. On the other hand, there is some evidence that Dostoevsky's own ideals in the Forties were Christian ones, at any rate before (and probably during) his brief and disastrous involvement in the Petrashevsky and Durov circles.

Admittedly, the Christianity of the young Dostoevsky was more secular than metaphysical. It might be characterized in a general way by faith in humanity, in Christ's image of man, and in the sacredness of art, all resting on a base of German idealism. A letter written in January 1840 to his brother provides some hints:[7]

> Homer (a legendary man who was maybe made flesh like Christ by God and sent to us) can be compared only to Christ, and not to Goethe. . . . In the *Iliad* Homer gave to the whole ancient world an organization of spiritual and earthly life, just as powerfully as Christ did for the new. . . . As a lyricist Victor Hugo has an Angelic Nature, and his poetry is of a childlike Christian tendency; and in this no-one can be compared with him,

neither Schiller (however Christian the poet Schiller may be), nor Shakespeare (as a lyricist – I've just read his Sonnets in French), nor Byron, nor Pushkin.

None the less his attachment to the image of the God-man proved the chief obstacle to Belinsky's attempts to convert him to a militantly atheistic and anti-Christian socialism:[8]

> 'It even touches me to look at him,' Belinsky suddenly interrupted his furious exclamations, as he turned to his friend and pointed at me. 'Every single time I mention Christ, his whole face changes, as if he wanted to cry.' He returned to the attack: 'Believe me, you naïve person, believe me if your Christ were born in our day, he would be the most inconspicuous and ordinary of men. He would just vanish, what with modern science and the modern movers of mankind.'

It is likely, therefore, that Dostoevsky's early radical sympathies, such as they were, were bound up with his Christian ideals, and that his remarks of 1876 about George Sand's Christianity also reflect his views as a young man (they certainly read like the observations of a man who had shared her ideals, and still held them for much the same reasons, albeit with a different emphasis). In the context of his enthusiastic remarks, it is of particular significance that he reserves the epithet of 'the great Christian' for Dickens. The question of what Dostoevsky meant by this may be left for the present, but if all these speculations are correct, it is confirmation that he saw him as a radical and – for the same reasons – a Christian; and that this was Dostoevsky's view in early years as well as in later life. Dickens's 'new word', of which Dostoevsky was aware almost from the start, lay in a distinctive compound of Christianity and radicalism, or perhaps, more simply, in his evangelism.

Dostoevsky's own statements can be made to go no further, if indeed they will go this far. But circumstantial evidence on its own makes it likely that by the autumn of 1844 (when he was writing *Poor Folk*) he knew Dickens's work at first hand. Although *Pickwick Papers* began to appear in England in 1836, it was not introduced to Russian readers until the end of 1838, when a translation (according to Katarsky a very free one) of the first quarter of the novel appeared in *Syn otechestva*. In 1840 both *Pickwick* and *Nicholas Nickleby* were translated in *Biblioteka dlia chteniia*. Kraevsky's journal, *Otechestvennye zapiski*, published a satisfactory translation of *Oliver Twist* in 1841; this gave rise to considerable critical interest in Dickens, and a translation of *Barnaby Rudge* (very accurate) followed in the same journal in 1841, of *Chuzzlewit* (less good) in 1844, and of *Dombey* in 1847–8. *The Old Curiosity Shop* was left to *Biblioteka dlia chteniia* (1843). Meanwhile, lesser works and extracts from the novels were appearing all over the place.[9] Dostoevsky was familiar with these journals; his letters contain several references to them. Balzac, whom he passionately admired and read, was published in those years in *Syn otechestva* and *Biblioteka dlia chteniia*. *Repertuar i Panteon*, which in 1845 issued a mutilated version of Dostoevsky's translation of *Eugénie Grandet*, also published *A Christmas Carol*. All in all, the chances that Dostoevsky failed to read some Dickens at this time are slight. In April 1844 Belinsky could observe, with an air of confidence, that the 'gifted writer' Dickens was well enough known in Russia for anyone to verify for himself that *Les Mystères de Paris* was a clumsy imitation of his work. 'Everyone has read his *Nicholas Nickleby*, *Oliver Twist*, *Barnaby Rudge*, and *Old Curiosity Shop*.' In the famous Annual Surveys of Russian Literature, Belinsky had been speaking with rising enthusiasm about Dickens as a social novelist, and in January 1845 he acclaimed *Martin Chuzzlewit* as perhaps the best of Dickens's novels, with its inexhaustible inventiveness, its variety of characters, its humour, and its style.[10]

Poor Folk

Dostoevsky announced to his brother on 30 September 1844, that he was completing a novel the size of *Eugénie Grandet*, and had begun to copy it out. In the event the announcement was premature, and on 24 March the following year, he wrote: 'I had completely finished it in about the month of November, but in December I suddenly thought I would do the whole thing over: I did it over and wrote it out. But in February I again began tidying up, smoothing out, putting in and taking out. About halfway through March, I was ready and satisfied.' On 4 May, he admitted he was correcting *Poor Folk* once again. (See letters nos. 26, 27, and 28, *Pis'ma*, vol. 1). In the absence of definite information, internal evidence from the novel must be the chief clue to Dostoevsky's knowledge of Dickens at this stage, and it will have to do double labour: it has to establish that he had read Dickens at the same time as it establishes that he was influenced by him. As Dostoevsky himself says (in the letter of 24 March), he did a great deal of reading during the writing of *Poor Folk*, and D. V. Grigorovich, with whom he was sharing a flat, records in his 'Literary Memoirs'[11] that 'a book would appear in Dostoevsky's hands the moment he stopped writing'. Of course, it was not only Dostoevsky's current reading that influenced his work, but since *Martin Chuzzlewit* was coming out in *Otechestvennye zapiski* during the last part of 1844 (a total of four parts, in the September, October, November, and December numbers), it is conceivable that it, too, along with Dickens's previous novels and those of the 'Sketches' which had been translated, helped to shape Dostoevsky's work.

Right at the beginning, Belinsky sensed the peculiar introspective nature of Dostoevsky's genius, and wrote about it in a review[12] of *Poor Folk*: 'it is apparent that Mr. Dostoevsky's talent is not satirical and not descriptive, but creative, and that its predominating trait is humour. He does not strike one with that knowledge of life and of the human heart which is given by experience and observation. No, he knows them, and knows them deeply, but his knowledge is *a priori*, and, therefore, purely poetic, creative.' Belinsky saw that Dostoevsky had followed Gogol's lead in portraying 'the down-trodden beings' of society, and had been influenced by his style; but he did not further probe the nature of Dostoevsky's '*a priori* knowledge', nor did he see that it was dependent on literary sources. N. N. Strakhov's later, incisive claim that *Poor Folk* was 'a correction of Gogol' helped to bring the question of its place in literary tradition to the centre of critical discussion.[13] Since then many critics have explored its aesthetic and ideological connections with Gogol's 'Petersburg Sketches', and in particular 'The Cloak', the story which has so terrible an effect on Dostoevsky's humble hero, Makar Devushkin. In accounting for Dostoevsky's 'correction' of Gogol, critics have referred to Pushkin or Balzac (Makar's devotion to another human being, or Dostoevsky's artistic methods); or to the sentimental novel of Karamzin and others (the lyrical effusions of Makar and Varvara); or to the Utopian Socialism of the 1840s (the concern for the ordinary man, the impossibility of happiness under the existing social system).[14] Most of these connections are of a rather general nature. The question to be considered here is what claim can be made for Dickens as the important corrective influence.

Dostoevsky depicts the same city-world of clerks, townspeople, obscure lodgings, and government officials as Gogol, and the forces governing it – poverty and dehumanizing institutions – are the same. But his picture is very different, and certainly, many elements of Dostoevsky's picture are more Dickensian than 'Gogol-esque': the joys of simple townspeople (the expedition to the theatre that Makar plans with such pleasure, or even his delighted exclamation, 'I went to buy some shoes, and bought such remarkable shoes'), or the sympathetic understanding of the struggles of the poor to keep some sort of self-respect. In Dostoevsky's Petersburg as in Dickens's London, the poor live, each with his own complicated history, in the crowded isolation of lodging-houses, and these strange, enclosed worlds contain new opportunities for humanity to assert and prove itself. Both authors recognize a new breed of city dwellers, whose happiness has to be found within the city-world, where they are threatened by the extinction of hope, and where the young and promising die. There is a certain fierce beauty in this new world, which the true townsman knows. The characters themselves in *Poor Folk* can be seen to fulfil symbolic functions analogous with some of Dickens's most characteristic figures. Makar writes in his letters about Gorshkov, whose family is starving as he waits for his case to come to trial. Like the Chancery prisoner from whom Mr Pickwick rents a room in the Fleet, he dies, a Victim of the Law (an analogy suggested by Katarsky); unlike him, he dies after his case has been heard and he has been vindicated – an ironic effect anticipatory of *Bleak House*. Pokrovsky, the legal parent of Varvara's student-friend (the actual father is Bykov), is – with his drunkenness and his cringing devotion to the hard-working, consumptive youth – an Improvident Father-figure, like the grandfather in *The Old Curiosity Shop*. The heroine, Varvara Dobroselova, lives – like those other representatives of Feminine Virtue, Kate Nickleby, Madeline Bray, and Ruth Pinch – in an uncomfortable position on the fringes of respectability; they work, in dependent situations, as governesses or companions, or they turn to needlework. To lose this position is to be plunged into sickness and destitution, or worse; seduction (by a Sir Mulberry Hawk) or an evil marriage (with a Gride) lie in wait for them (the bogyman Bykov attempts both). And as for the hero, the timid, self-conscious Makar Devushkin, he is brother to Dickens's Shabby-Genteel Man who keeps losing buttons from his coat, while with his unselfishness and aspiration for happiness, he is a figure of Goodness and Humility like Tim Linkinwater and Tom Pinch.

But were Tim Linkinwater and his kind a means for Dostoevsky to discover man, in the way he indicated Falstaff and Chichikov had been? Consider the characters Dostoevsky said were to be found in almost every novel by Dickens: 'humbled persons, righteous but yielding, downtrodden, foolish but seeing' (*prinizhennye litsa, spravedlivye, no ustupaiushchie, iurodlivye i zabitye*).[15] Some of the words are worth pondering. The first of them is rather less strong than *unizhennye*, the word Dostoevsky used in the title of the book generally known as *The Insulted and Injured*, and which could be translated as 'humiliated'. *Prinizhennye* has connotations of submissiveness and acceptance, with an underlying notion of man brought down to a norm. *Iurodlivye* or (in the singular) *iurodlivyi* comes from *iurodivyi*, which can refer to a man who is just simple-minded, but generally one who has visionary powers and may even be saintly. This word has a strong association with the Holy Fool traditional in Russia. The change in the word breaks the specific Russian connection, and weakens the meaning, as though Dostoevsky wanted to describe a disposition rather than an attribute. Perhaps, too, he was seeking to form a hybrid with the etymologically related word, *urodlivyi*, meaning 'ugly'. These terms with their high moral colouring suggest that Dostoevsky's vision of reality was no ordinary one. And certainly the application of these words to the characters of both authors is obvious. But any question of influence is not very interesting here if it is supposed to operate between specific figures. Dostoevsky's poor have recognizable counterparts in Dickens, but their labels do not begin to indicate their complexities and depths of feeling and behaviour (for instance, that whole episode in which Varvara and old Pokrovsky save what money they can, in order to buy a set of Pushkin's works for the student). And in the absence of any very detailed similarity, it is dangerous to suppose Dickens's humble characters acted as a revelation of reality.

The question is further complicated by the translations Dostoevsky is likely to have read. The Russian version of *Martin Chuzzlewit* was substantially accurate, whereas *Nicholas Nickleby* was considerably abridged in *Biblioteka dlia chteniia*[16] and many of Dickens's most characteristic and original devices and touches were obliterated. Dickens keeps several plots moving simultaneously and continually switches from one to the other; the fragmentation of modern life is reflected in the telling of the story. The translator reorders the narrative in conventional way, and develops one strand of the story more fully before taking up another. Dickens's biting satire disappears; the clergyman who says 'It is sinful to rebel' in the opening chapter of the novel is lost. In the original novel Linkinwater speaks about the hump-backed boy who cultivates flowers in old blacking bottles in his attic window:

> At night, when he sees my candle, he draws back his curtain,
> and leaves it so, till I am in bed. It seems such company to him to
> know that I am there, that I often sit in my window for an
> hour or more, that he may see I am still awake. . . . The night
> will not be long coming . . . when he will sleep, and never wake
> again on earth. We have never so much as shaken hands in all
> our lives; and yet I shall miss him like an old friend. Are there
> any country flowers that could interest me like these, do you
> think? Or do you suppose that the withering of a hundred kinds
> of the choicest flowers that blow, called by the hardest Latin
> names that were ever invented, would give me one fraction of the
> pain that I shall feel when those old jugs and bottles are swept
> away as lumber! Country! . . . Don't you know that I couldn't
> have such a court under my bed-room window, anywhere, but
> in London? (ch. 40)

In the translation Tim Linkinwater is simply made to say that anything you can get in the country you can also get in the town, and the hump-backed boy with the poignant little history is replaced by a neighbour who merely cultivates peonies in her flower pots.

The significant influence, if it exists, has to do with the use the two authors make of their characters. It concerns the whole structure within which the characters act (and of this enough survives even in the translation of *Nickleby* for it to be possible to pursue the question). Dostoevsky's picture of man in *Poor Folk* is self-consciously different from Gogol's in 'The Cloak'. Makar is profoundly disturbed by the image of himself he sees in Akaky Akakievich ('Why, after that it is impossible to live in peace in your corner . . .'), and challenges the whole purpose of Gogol's art: 'And why write something like that? For what is it necessary? Well, is any reader going to make me a cloak as a result of it? Or buy me some new shoes? No, Varenka. He'll read it and ask for the sequel. Sometimes you will hide and hide, and keep what they haven't got hold of a secret . . . and here all your civic and personal life goes about in books; everything is printed, read, derided and censured.'[17] In Pushkin's 'Station-Master' he finds an image of himself that he can accept, and which is, moreover, an image of all mankind. This, too, is Dostoevsky's aim: to reveal the universal man concealed in an ordinary titular councillor. His early experiences as an author are dramatized in *The Insulted and Injured* (1861) in the person of Vania; when Vania reads aloud his first novel to some friends, one of them – the kind old Ikhmenev – is disappointed that it is not high literature, but grants that for all that 'it grips the heart; makes you understand and remember what is going on around you; makes you know that even the last and most downtrodden of men is also a man and his name is my brother'.[18] Gogol's picture of man, his mental life reduced to lines of script and an overcoat, was alienating. Dostoevsky wants to reconcile man with himself and his fellow man. In this he acknowledges Pushkin rather than Gogol as a model. But Dostoevsky does not seek simply to evoke sympathy; he displays it in action. The moments in which the characters in *Poor Folk* recognize their common humanity and reach out to help each other provide some of the chief climaxes of the story. The whole novel is concerned, in all sorts of ways, with philanthropy. And here the closeness of his concerns to Dickens's should be apparent.

It is a commonplace that Dickens (in his early novels) hopes the problems of society can vanish if men will only do their duty and be generous. In the words of Orwell: 'If men would behave decently the world would be decent. Naturally this calls for a few characters who are in positions of authority and *do* behave decently.'[19] Dickens does not place all his reliance on the Pickwicks, Garlands, Cheerybles, old Martin Chuzzlewits and so forth; he hopes that honest, industrious, poor, humble men (and sometimes, when he is off guard, the 'umble poor) can themselves do a certain amount to secure the reward that is due to them. To protect the humble virtues he is prepared to send Little Nell deep into England's rural past, or to sanctify the back-parlour behind the instrument-maker's shop in *Dombey*. Subsequently *Little Dorrit* proves to be the novel in which he adopts the outlook of such characters most consistently, and where it grows into a vision of a transformed society. But already in the early novels he reaches towards a vision of what these people, left to themselves, might achieve, and of what the pressures on them are. *Nicholas Nickleby*, in particular, is concerned with the attempts of men living in towns to re-form some sort of community. Miss La Creevy becomes one of its founders:[20]

> One of the many to whom, from straitened circumstances, a consequent inability to form the associations they would wish, and a disinclination to mix with the society they could obtain, London is as complete a solitude as the plains of Syria, the humble artist had pursued her lonely but contented way for many years; and, until the peculiar misfortunes of the Nickleby family attracted her attention, had made no friends, though brimfull of the friendliest feelings to all mankind.

The Nicklebys, with the distinction of a decayed fortune behind them, qualify for a privileged position; Newman Noggs is a valuable adjunct because of his knowledge of the world; Smike is salvaged and made a public charge; and eventually Tim Linkinwater, who is at the centre of another embryonic community, joins forces with them. But Dickens is afraid to stand for very long on resignation and poverty, especially in the early novels. He hopes that the whole of society can be transformed by the simple substitution of good men for bad, and hence that his humble men can be rewarded for their patience. It is here that his vision of man in the city-world is threatened by the fantasy of the year-round Christmas.

Despite the Good Rich Men and the embarrassed handling of class relations, Dickens does a fair amount to make his fragile communities seem interesting and plausible. They are a natural response of men to their isolated conditions of life and work. They are a proof of their essential dignity, that common denominator between men, to which even Mrs Todgers attains 'among the sordid strivings of her life'. They contain certain possibilities of joy (play-going, or Tom Pinch's books, or steak-and-kidney pudding) or contentment, in a world in which otherwise the chief pleasure to appear is the contagious delight of the author in acting out his own creation. Then, too, on Dickens's tame men, rests part of the burden of opposing constructive action to the forces of self-interest that are disrupting society. The alternative, rebellion, is always a danger, and it takes many forms: Nicholas's recourse to violence (justified) in order to abolish a specific social abuse at Dotheboys Hall; the rioting of the mobs (senseless) in *Barnaby Rudge*; and more interestingly, the despair that overcomes Nicholas in the face of the evil of the world: 'how many died in soul, and had no chance

27

of life; how many who could scarcely go astray, be they vicious as they would, turned haughtily from the crushed and stricken wretch who could scarce do otherwise . . . how much injustice, misery, and wrong, there was, and yet how the world rolled on, from year to year, alike careless and indifferent, and no man seeking to remedy or redress it'.[21] In a world like this, resignation and kindness can even be seen to have a certain internal tension, giving them the force of a positive option. Even though this is nowhere adequately expressed (at least not in the early novels), Dickens comes some way towards a direct statement with Tom Pinch, to whom he has denied the love of Mary Graham: 'It is sorrowful to me to contemplate my dream, which I always knew was a dream, even when it first presented itself; but the realities about me are not to blame. They are the same as they were. My sister, my sweet companion, who makes this place so dear, is she less devoted to me. . . ? My old friend John . . . is he less cordial to me?'[22] With or without psychological complexity, the community of the humble is an attempt to counter the evil of the world, to re-establish some sort of norm in a society of broken-down families and rapacious self-interest.

To all this *Poor Folk* is closely related: it is about the needs of the disinherited men of society. Dostoevsky hopes that in the city-world of St Petersburg, with the special opportunities it gives men for knowing one another, there is some basis that can serve for the regeneration of mankind. Makar has spent his life 'in solitude, in deprivation, without joy, without a friendly word of greeting, in corners rented from strangers'.[23] The chance friendship between him and Varvara becomes, as it unfolds in their letters, a pattern of what men could achieve and of the difficulties in their way (the epistolary form, we note, is true to the loneliness of the city man and to his intensified imagination). The significance of the relationship is neatly expressed in one of Makar's letters:

Because I got to know you, I began, first of all, to know myself better and to love you, whereas before you, my angel, I was alone and as if asleep rather than alive on earth. They – my wrong-doers – said that even my person was indecent and despised me, and so I began to despise myself; said I was thick, and indeed I thought I was thick. But when you came to me you lit up all my dark life, so that my heart and soul lit up; my spirit was at rest; and I learned that I am no worse than the others, that it is only that I in no way shine, have no polish, have no style; but, none the less, I am a man; with a heart and mind I am a man. But now I feel that I am persecuted by fate, and that, degraded by fate I have given myself to denying my own dignity . . . (pp. 172f.)

Dostoevsky believes that even in men as oppressed by material circumstances as Gogol's Akaky Akakievich, the need for human affection cannot be destroyed. Not that Dostoevsky would deny that, in Nabokov's words, a man's cloak could be his mistress, but he is more concerned with what a man can achieve than with what he can be reduced to. As Makar enters into Varvara's trials, makes great sacrifices to find small pleasures for her, and gives his last twenty kopecks to a man in greater misery than himself, he discovers and asserts his human dignity. He travels the distance between a Smike ('he was an altered being; he had an object now; and that object was, to show his attachment to the only person – that person a stranger – who had treated him, not to say with kindness, but like a human creature') and a Pinch ('So long as I heard that he was happy, and he heard that I was . . . we could both bear, without one impatient or complaining thought, a great deal more than ever we have had to endure').[24] For Dostoevsky, at this stage, the only real basis of equality and of any worthwhile society lies in the mutual recognition of human dignity (it is not until his later fiction that the vision of society as a specifically Christian brotherhood emerges, by which time he is more pessimistic than cautious as to the need of the urbanized Russian for reconciliation, and brotherhood is in the nature of an ideal against which to measure man's alienation). The whole structure of society made it very difficult for the poor to preserve their dignity, and unlikely that the rich would pay any attention to them. As Makar's difficulties increase, and he is less and less able to help Varvara, he turns in despair to drink – or else to rebellion, for he knows that with his concern for his fellow man, he has come closer to true human dignity than the inhabitants of the 'gilded palaces' (p. 181). Much as he is frightened of his 'free thinking' he is even driven (not unlike Nicholas Nickleby, and like him in the city streets) to question the whole order of the universe (p. 177): 'Why is it always happening that the good man lives in desolation [zapusten'e] while happiness presses itself on some other man?'

In a preface contributed to a translation of *Notre Dame de Paris* in 1862, Dostoevsky speaks of the 'restoration of fallen man' and the 'justification of the pariahs of society' as the basic idea of all nineteenth-century art.[25] For this it is necessary that the rich and powerful should be aware of the poor and should help them. An important difference from Dickens is that Dostoevsky is consistently aware of the difficulty of charity. Instead of serving to express *common* humanity, it can enforce the inequality of men. Makar describes the subscription that was being raised for one of his friends (p. 154): 'for every penny they gave him, so to speak, an official inspection. They thought they were giving him their pennies for nothing. Oh no! They were paying to have a poor man shown to them. Nowadays even charity seems to be done queerly – or maybe, who knows, that's how it was always done.' And Dostoevsky dramatizes far more effectively the limits of what charity can do. Makar speaks of a boy he has seen begging (p. 180): ' "Go 'way! Be off! None of your tricks!" – that's what he hears from everybody.'[26] This sort of voice Dickens does capture; its effect is to make us want to compensate for it with a great outflow of sympathy. But there are other voices, holding little hope for the regeneration of society, and these Dickens must not have wanted to hear (with Jo and with the brickmakers in *Bleak House*, Dickens puts some of these other voices to use). Makar describes beggars who repeat their phrase in 'a long, drawn-out, inured, routine, true pauper's way', and adds that to them it is less painful to give nothing. There is also the boy who does not approach everyone but addresses Makar: 'Master, give a penny, in Christ's name!' speaking in such an uncustomary, rough, terrible voice, that Makar recalls, 'I shuddered from some terrible feeling, but didn't give the penny: I hadn't one' (p. 180). True philanthropy, resting on respect for human dignity and on mutual awareness, is almost a luxury.

Makar is rescued from despair when his head-of-department, suddenly realizing his situation, gives him a hundred-rouble note. The circumstances through which Makar and the head come to see each other as fellow men are finely brought out. Makar is called before him to be reprimanded for a mistake, and on his way in, catches a glimpse of himself in the mirror and is horrified. Just as he is asked for an explanation, one of his last remaining buttons, which for weeks has been hanging by a thread, comes off (it 'tore loose, leapt away, jumped up . . . jangled, and rolled' right to the feet of the head-of-department). Makar throws himself after the button, picks it up, tries to stick it back on his coat, and as he stands there, smiling in stunned horror, he hears the head making enquiries about him of the other people present, and then addressing him:

'Well, the whole thing must be copied out again. Devushkin, come here. Copy it again without any mistakes. Oh, and listen –'
Here His Excellency turns to the others, gives various orders, and everyone goes off. As soon as they have gone, His Excellency hurriedly pulls out a pocket-book and from it, a hundred-rouble note. 'Here', he says, 'What I'm able to do – regard it as you wish –' And puts it in my hand. I . . . shuddered; all my soul was shaken; I don't know what was happening to me; I wanted to seize his hand. And he blushed all over . . . yes – and here I am not departing one hair's breadth from the truth . . .
– he took my unworthy hand and shook it. Took it and shook it, as though with an equal, a general like himself. 'Go', he said. 'What I'm able to do – don't make any mistakes, and now, let's forget it' [*grekh popolam* – literally 'the sin is shared']. (p. 187)

This is very close to the vigorous hand-shaking and rapid talking that accompany the cash-handouts of the brothers Cheeryble.[27] But the Cheerybles are shameless. The achievement here, the way in which Makar and his chief manage to assert their belief in human dignity over and above the circumstances dividing them, has no equivalent in Dickens. There is not just an awareness of one man's hardship, but a mutual revelation of two persons.

It is because of a belief in the fundamental equality of all that Dickens and Dostoevsky portray ordinary men and wish to regenerate society. Where Dostoevsky is so superior is in his ability to dramatize this equality, and thus to remove all barriers to the sympathy and understanding with which meaningful charity begins. In the end neither Makar's devotion nor the hundred-rouble note can prevent Varvara from marrying Bykov, her persecutor. Yet what defeats Makar is not so much the Russian social system, nor the impotence of charity, as the injustice of *any* society, in which there will always be strong and weak men, and in which men's likes and dislikes do not fall into neat patterns. It is conceivable that, in a more just society, Varvara would not be driven into marrying Bykov in order to escape from poverty. Makar's misfortune is of a more universal significance.

As he comes to know Varvara, he discovers his love for her; but all the while her letters to him breathe little more than gratitude, friendliness, and pleasure at having someone to confide in. This is part of the irremediable injustice of the world. Makar is a man in whom the inhabitants of the 'gilded palaces' can and should recognize themselves. Because he can be seen as an equal in his spiritual and emotional life, the physical hardships he suffers are the more intolerable. The concern we are encouraged to adopt is of a direct man-to-man kind; it is an extension, a heightening, of the charitable relation.

Dickens never quite sees his humble characters in terms of universal fate (at least till he comes to Joe in *Great Expectations*). Smike, with his unhappy love for Kate Nickleby, serves a purpose close to Makar's, but throughout, remains a grotesque. Tom Pinch is a somewhat more interesting case. Despite (or because of) Tom's self-sacrificing love, Mary Graham marries young Martin Chuzzlewit, and for Dickens, Tom's personal drama makes him an object of special concern (characteristically, Dickens endeavours to make compensation to him by giving him an organ to play on and a role of favourite uncle). What is seriously wrong is that Dickens does not face up to the issues, moral, physical, and social, involved in Mary's preference for Martin. Because the sense of Tom's moral superiority is so strong and his funny looks are so soon forgotten, it is easily concluded that the essential disability is one of class. And because Dickens does not acknowledge this, he seems to be willing, in fact if not in intention, to countenance a society which, by its very structure, debars some of its members from certain areas of feeling and experience. It is revealing that the equivalent in Dickens to Makar's 'with a heart and mind I am a man' is Tom Pinch's assertion that he has 'as good a right to common consideration as another'.[28] Dickens prefers not to put his egalitarianism to the test, as though he were afraid it might pose too great a challenge to his society. The counterpart of his failure is his escape into fantasy when he presents his vision of a transformed society.

Poor Folk is distinguished by its aesthetic self-consciousness. In the questions Dostoevsky raises about the purpose of art, and about charity and humility, his novel refers in a remarkable way back to itself and outwards to its readers. Ultimately, it is not so much the existence of humble people that Dostoevsky puts his faith in, as the existence of an art which increases mutual awareness and helps men to achieve humility. Like Pushkin's Samson Vyrin ('The Station-Master')

Makar can be seen as a paradigm of human and moral worth. Because of Pushkin and Dostoevsky, because their kind of art was possible, and because it was accessible to all, there was – as is implicit in *Poor Folk* – hope for Russian society. And of course, Dickens's art was of this same sort, without the Dostoevskian awareness.

It can be seen that, despite certain limitations and prejudices in Dickens, he and Dostoevsky started with a similar vision of society. Both saw a resigned humility and a timid sociability among men faced with the crowded solitude of city life, and hoped that these qualities were a basis for regeneration. They were united by their consciousness of the wrongness of society, their wish to change it, their hope it could be transformed through greater mutual awareness and charity. Hence, society was for them more than Balzac's vast devouring machine, with its ruthless exploiters and silently suffering victims. At the same time, unlike George Sand, they had no ideal schemes based on the teachings of a Saint-Simon or a Pierre Leroux to put into effect, and no daughters of the aristocracy to marry noble-spirited scions of the working classes. Human dignity had to triumph in spite of and through the existing social structure. The transformation they envisaged was in the first instance a change in man's state of feeling – leading, in the one, by an over-hasty process, to the myth of Christmas all the year round, and in the other, to that complex understanding which passed between a man and his employer. The closeness of the two authors' basic interests are borne out by some words Dostoevsky had to say about the good heart in the 'Feuilleton' of 1847 which also contained his first reference to Dickens (*Stat'i*, p. 11): 'only in the presence of generalized interests, in sympathy for the mass of society and for its direct, immediate requirements, and not in slumber, not in indifference, from which the mass is falling apart, can [a man's] treasure, his capital, his good heart, be polished into a precious, real shining diamond.' Their 'philanthropic tendency' had to do with the attempt to restore the dignity, equality, and brotherhood of mankind, and to transform society from within. It was basically an evangelical concern.

But was Dostoevsky influenced by Dickens, and had he read him before writing *Poor Folk*? In the Russia of Nicholas I, where political and social reform could not be openly discussed, Dickens's type of social novel would have been of obvious interest to Dostoevsky.[29] If we were certain that, by the time of his work on *Poor Folk*, he had read Dickens's novels, we could say without hesitation that they helped him to find an escape from the repression and alienation of Gogol's world, and hence to find what kind of novel he was going to write. It was not so much any particular one of Dickens's humble men that would have impressed him, as the whole community of them. None of the similarities between characters and episodes are, however, so detailed or systematic or distinctive as to show on their own that he had to have read Dickens. Whether one can speak here of an influence rests in the end on external evidence, and this, as was shown at the outset, is not as it stands conclusive. But whether Dostoevsky had read Dickens before writing *Poor Folk*, or started to read him immediately after (at any rate sometime before April 1847), he must have recognized how close their aims as social novelists were. And when in 1876 he called Dickens a 'great Christian', it was surely not only because Dickens had portayed humble characters, but because he had attempted to make their outlook a basis for a new brotherhood, in which man's thirst for equality would be satisfied.

Notes

1 Nos. 16 and 27, *Pis'ma*, vol. 1; no. 14, *Pis'ma*, vol. 2; no. 816, *Pis'ma*, vol. 4.
2 *Fyodor Dostoyevsky* (London, 1921), p. 203.
3 *Stat'i*, pp. 160ff.
4 *Stat'i*, pp. 14f.
5 No. 349, *Pis'ma*, vol. 2.
6 *Dnevnik pisatelia* (Paris, 1951), vol. 2, p. 234.
7 No. 16, *Pis'ma*, vol. 1.
8 'Old People', *Diary of a Writer* (1873). *Dnevnik pisatelia*, vol. 1, p. 191.
9 See Iu. V. Fridlender and I. M. Katarsky, *Charl'z Dikkens: Bibliografiia*, pp. 40–85.
10 *Polnoe sobranie sochinenii* (Moscow, 1953–9), vol. 5, p. 585; vol. 8, pp. 85, 184, 484f.
11 In *F. M. Dostoevsky v vospominaniiakh sovremennikov*, ed. A. S. Dolinin (Moscow, 1964), vol. 1, pp. 130f.
12 *Polnoe sobranie sochinenii*, vol. 9, pp. 550f.
13 *V pamiat' F. M. Dostoevskogo* (St Petersburg, 1881), p. 21.
14 See the discussions by R. L. Jackson, Kirpotin, and Mochulsky. There is a particularly illuminating analysis of Dostoevsky's use of sentimental and naturalist modes in V. V. Vinogradov, *Evoliutsiia russkogo naturalizma: Gogol' i Dostoevsky* (Leningrad, 1929).
15 In the second of the articles on George Sand, *Diary of a Writer* (1876).
16 Vols 38 and 39 (1840).

17 *Poor Folk*, p. 146 (in *Sobranie sochinenii*, vol. 1).
18 Part I, ch. 6.
19 *Critical Essays* (London, 1946), p. 10.
20 *Nickleby*, ch. 20, p. 246. Unless otherwise indicated, the essential meaning survived in the translation.
21 *Nickleby*, ch. 53, p. 693. Considerably simplified in the translation.
22 *Chuzzlewit*, ch. 50, p. 768.
23 *Poor Folk*, pp. 84f.
24 *Nickleby*, ch. 12, p. 143; *Chuzzlewit*, ch. 9, p. 136.
25 See *Stat'i*, p. 526.
26 '*Proch'! ubiraisia! shalish'!*'
27 For example *Nickleby*, ch. 35.
28 *Poor Folk*, p. 173; *Chuzzlewit*, ch. 24, p. 391.
29 Dickens and radicalism again seem to go together in *What is to be Done?* (1863), but its author, Chernyskevsky, responds only to the crudest aspects of Dickensian good humour and characterization.

3

Breakdown of brotherhood

Kind hearts or false ones

In the 'Petersburg Feuilleton' of 1847 in which Dostoevsky first mentions Dickens, he exclaims with mock irony over the disappearance of melodramatic figures from the world, and the consequent difficulty of telling bad men from good. By way of illustration he conjures up a certain Iulian Mastakovich, a man in his fifties, of respectable station, who plans to wed a seventeen-year-old girl. This character, it appears, is a sensualist and hypocrite: while he enjoys the prospect of possessing a young, innocent bride, he is reluctant to give up his visits to an attractive widow he is supposedly advising out of kindness of heart in a certain legal matter.[1] He has a family likeness with Mr Pecksniff from *Martin Chuzzlewit*; moreover, two tales into which he is introduced deal with some of the same questions as does this novel by Dickens.

'A Weak Heart' (1848) is set like most of Dostoevsky's early works in the world of poor government workers. Vasia Shumkov, a three-hundred-rouble-a-year copying clerk, shares lodgings with his colleague and close friend, Arkady. Vasia has been trying to console a young girl abandoned by the man she loved, falls in love with her himself, and when the story opens, on New Year's eve, they have decided to marry. It so happens that he has undertaken some supplementary copying for his head, Iulian Mastakovich, and is supposed to hand over an assignment in three days' time. Having fallen behind in his duties while courting Liza, Vasia is overwhelmed at once by his new-found happiness and the crushing load of work, panics, and grows so desperately confused that just before the deadline he goes out of his mind.

Vasia, who is afflicted with crippled legs, is kin to Tom Pinch ('an ungainly, awkward-looking man, extremely shortsighted, and prematurely bald') – the governing characteristic of both is gratitude.

36

He cannot get over the kindness of Iulian Mastakovich, who spotted his talent and gave him a clerical job (at the bottom of the Russian system of ranks). He feels incredibly fortunate to have the friendship of Arkady: 'I don't know why you liked me so much. Yes, Arkady, do you know your love has even been destroying me? You know, often when going to bed and thinking about you (because I always think about you when I go to sleep) I have been overcome with tears, and my heart has trembled because – well, because you like me so much, and there was no way to ease my heart, no way to thank you.'[2] The more extreme outpourings of Tom Pinch's good heart were omitted in the *Otechestvennye zapiski* translation, for instance his exclamation to young Martin: 'everybody who comes here . . . is more considerate and affectionate to me than I should have any right to hope, if I were the most sanguine creature in the world; or should have any power to express if I were the most eloquent. It really overpowers me. But trust me . . . that I am not ungrateful; that I never forget; and that, if I can ever prove the truth of my words to you, I will.' Nevertheless Tom remains uncritically admiring of his employer and friends. He comes from a genteel family (his grandmother was a housekeeper), and having been educated by Pecksniff at a reduced rate, he lets himself be shamelessly exploited.[3] Similarly Vasia might expect to make four hundred roubles a year for the extra work he has been doing, but we learn that after five months Iulian Mastakovich has just given him fifty roubles, and, so, excites Vasia's enthusiastic gratitude and at the same time tremendous guilt for fear he is not measuring up to the trust placed in him.

Two kinds of 'good heart' appear in Dostoevsky's little story: one concerned with appearances and with good deeds, the other overflowing with good will and feeling (so much so as to threaten its grasp of reality). Vasia is given a chance to have his love but fails to defend it. While his failure has something to do with the social order, there is a hint that the basic cause lies even deeper than for Makar Devushkin – it is rooted in his very being. He feels 'guilty *before himself,* in relation to fate'. Arkady says to him: 'You're kind, tender, but weak, unforgivably weak . . . Besides, you are a dreamer, and that too is bad: you can lose yourself, brother! I know what you want. You would like Iulian Mastakovich to be so beside himself at your getting married, that, out of joy, he would maybe even give a ball. . . . Since you are happy you want everyone, absolutely everyone, all at once, to be happy. It is hard and painful for you to be happy on your own.' Gratitude becomes a complex and interesting emotion in 'A Weak Heart'; in contrast, in *Martin Chuzzlewit* it remains a conventional virtue. Even though Tom has to suppress his love for Mary, Dickens pretends that his gratitude to her and to Martin for giving him their friendship can amount to perfect happiness: 'Martin and Mary had taken him aside before dinner, and spoken to him so heartily of the time to come: laying such fervent stress upon the trust they had in his completion of their felicity: that Tom was positively moved to tears.' Dickens comforts himself with the easy reflection that virtue finds its own reward, and makes himself an apologist for a marriage based largely on social considerations. But Dickens did formulate the problem of the over-grateful heart, even if his solution is hardly satisfactory.[4]

In 'A Christmas Tree and a Wedding' (1848) Iulian Mastakovich makes another appearance, this time at a children's Christmas party where, as a man of influence, he is fussed over and courted by the parents. One of the little girls, an eleven-year-old, is the daughter of a rich capitalist, and when Iulian Mastakovich overhears some of the guests whispering about the three hundred thousand roubles that have been set aside for her dowry, he makes friends with the girl's father, and then goes into a neighbouring room, where the narrator hears him making calculations in a stage whisper:[5]

> Three hundred – three hundred . . . eleven – twelve – thirteen – and so forth. Sixteen makes five years! Let's take 4 per cent, making twelve, times five equals sixty, and on top of these sixty there will be – well, say, in five years, four hundred. Yes. But he'll not keep it at 4 per cent, the scoundrel. Maybe he gets 8 or 10 per cent. So five hundred, let's say five hundred, that at any rate is certain.

His calculations complete, Iulian Mastakovich goes to the girl, who is playing with the son of a poor governess, and tries to make friends with her. In terror she clings to the little boy. Iulian Mastakovich leans over to kiss her, and both children burst into tears. He chases the boy away and pursues him; the boy takes refuge under the table, from which Iulian Mastakovich tries to shoo him out with a handkerchief. Just then the host comes up and proceeds to speak about the governess's child in the hope that Iulian Mastakovich will exert his influence to get him a place in a certain school. Peevishly Iulian Mastakovich refuses. Five years later Iulian Mastakovich marries the girl, now sixteen, and possessed of five hundred thousand roubles.

Mercenary marriages are important in *Martin Chuzzlewit*. In one scene Jonas enquires into the extent of Merry's dowry, and having received an answer, remains silent for some fifteen minutes: 'during the whole of that time [he] appeared to be steadily engaged in subjecting some given amount to the operation of every known rule in figures; adding to it, taking from it, multiplying it, reducing it by long and short division, working it by the rule-of-three direct and inversed; exchange or barter; practice; simple interest; compound interest; and other means of arithmetical calculation. The result of these labours appeared to be satisfactory.' Although he lacks a principal on which to base his calculations, Mr Pecksniff indulges in a similar speculation with regard to Mary Graham: 'Let the old man say what he would, Mr Pecksniff knew he had a strong affection for her. . . . That he had ever really sworn to leave her nothing in his will, Mr Pecksniff greatly doubted. . . . "Then," said Mr Pecksniff, "what if I married her! What," repeated Mr Pecksniff, sticking up his hair and glancing at his bust by Spoker: "What if, making sure of his approval first – he is nearly imbecile, poor gentleman – I married her!"' Combining a paternal role with a suitor's, Mr Pecksniff forces his unwelcome attentions on Mary in the course of a walk, causing her to burst into tears (he even inclines 'his flabby face to hers' and kisses her). In the church a little later Mary confides to Tom what has happened, just when Pecksniff chances to be lying concealed behind one of the pews. In consequence, Mr Pecksniff feels impelled to discharge 'his duty to society' and to part with Tom's services.[6]

In *Poor Folk* what made the community of well-intentioned men an impossibility was chiefly the conflict between their aspirations and the world they had to live in. In the subsequent tales, Dostoevsky explored impediments lying inside man: the denial of the aggressive instincts that goes with humility might turn into a death-wish; benevolence had no meaning for some men except as a cover for self-interest. Because of the similarities *Martin Chuzzlewit* offers with 'A Weak Heart' and 'A Christmas Tree and a Wedding' it is possible and even likely Dickens helped Dostoevsky to define the problems. The similarities are not of a kind which would allow one to conclude that Dostoevsky was reacting against Dickens's facile judgments and solutions (although the cynical Christmas tale is perhaps of some significance). The difference in Dostoevsky's method was probably more important. He liked to give his characters the fullest test he could in order to find what they could do and what could come of their outlook on the world. This does not mean that his method was necessarily more realistic; on the contrary, it means he often placed his characters in quite exceptional situations. But, in consequence, he was rarely over-optimistic about what any one person could achieve.

New characters and experiments

There is surely something artistically unsatisfactory about most of Dostoevsky's other writings after *The Double* and up to *Notes from the Underground*. A discussion of influence in this period is interesting not so much for what it tells us about the writings as for what it can show about the workings of the influence before and afterwards. One reason for Dostoevsky's difficulties after his first critical success – and the undeserved critical failure of *The Double* – had to do with his desperate attempt to consolidate his position in the world of letters. And after his term of imprisonment and exile in Siberia, he had to begin again the task of establishing his literary reputation, at the same time as he placated the censors. Before and after Siberia he was casting around for new themes and for a new manner. Several of the works he produced are more or less successful exercises in the manner of Gogol, Balzac, Hoffmann, Schiller, and – Dickens. 'Exercise' is the operative word if we consider, for example, the preface of 'A Little Hero', a short story Dostoevsky wrote in 1849 when he was incarcerated in the Peter-and-Paul Fortress; in its delicacy and lyricism the story bears no trace of his ordeal. The preface (which Dostoevsky omitted after the story was first published in 1857) is written in a somewhat different vein, which Katarsky[7] has observed is close to Dickens in 'The Cricket on the Hearth' and elsewhere in *The Christmas Books*. A short quotation will suffice for illustration: 'Even our fireplace seemed to rejoice that we had grown still, as if to listen to its merry crackling; and it glowed so willingly, so merrily, for our pleasure, that, in truth, it was just like a welcoming host when good men are visiting him and he, for joy, cannot do enough to make them feel warm and at ease and willing to stay.'

The Dickens manner or style was a distraction for Dostoevsky during his prison years (we recall again the report that Dickens's novels were the only ones to interest him in the Omsk convict-prison). It was also a danger, as we can see from his comic novels, *The Uncle's Dream* and *The Village of Stepanchikovo* (1859), which he wrote after his release while he was still exiled and serving as a soldier in Semipalatinsk. In a letter written at this time (no. 97, *Pis'ma*, i) he expressed a fear that it might prove difficult to publish something 'the size of Dickens's novels'; *Stepanchikovo* is probably a fragment of the projected work. *The Uncle's Dream* is particularly important because it provides graphic evidence that Dostoevsky had read *Dombey and Son* and found the melodramatic Edith Dombey puzzling. (He was not the only writer to be struck by her – George Eliot drew on Edith for Mrs Transome in *Felix Holt*.) Dostoevsky's tale is concerned with the attempt of a petty tyrant of provincial society, Maria Aleksandrovna Moskaleva, to get the decrepit old Prince K. to marry her daughter Zina. She more or less kidnaps the senile Prince, who has come from St Petersburg to visit his estates; persuades him that he needs a young and devoted wife to look after him; forces Zina (who is in love with a poor, consumptive school-teacher) to agree to marry the Prince; and with a bit of management gets the Prince to make a proposal. There are various complications due to the intrigues of the other ladies in the town, spies hiding behind doors, and so on, but Maria Aleksandrovna's undoing is a relation of the Prince's, who persuades him that his proposal to Zina was nothing but an enchanting dream (a device possibly suggested by *Pickwick Papers*, ch. 8). The Prince, feeling he has made a terrible mistake, seizes at this explanation and is readily persuaded of its truth. When the town's leading inhabitants and scandalmongers are gathered at Maria Aleksandrovna's, she reveals that the Prince has an important announcement to make; to her dismay he proceeds to describe his 'dream'. The feeble-mindedness of the Prince is effectively proved, and the marriage becomes an impossibility.

Katarsky has convincingly demonstrated that another intriguing and ambitious mother, Mrs Skewton, and her unhappy daughter, Edith, were important influences in this tale. Maria Aleksandrovna shares Mrs Skewton's enthusiasm for the Middle Ages: ' "Oh!" cried Mrs Skewton, with a faded little scream of rapture, "the Castle is charming! associations of the Middle Ages – and all that – which is so truly exquisite. Don't you dote upon the Middle Ages, Mr Carker?" ' This becomes: 'Oh, Prince, how I love everything to do with chivalry! The castles, the castles – the life of the Middle Ages. The troubadours,

the heralds, the tournaments.'[8] Mrs Skewton's physical characteristics
are assigned to the Prince, who is all paint and spare parts. Cousin
Feenix, with his wandering mind and his sense of knowing everybody,
could be another influence on him (the Prince claims to have known
Beethoven and Byron, but this turns out to be a trick of his confused
memory). A comparison of Dostoevsky's characters with the originals
does, I think, bring out that there is something wooden and lifeless
about Prince K. and Maria Aleksandrovna. Part of the reason is surely
that he did not know what he was portraying (probably a result of his
long isolation from society), and relied on Mrs Skewton while sacri-
ficing everything that gave this figure from Regency England indivi-
duality and life. At the same time, he simply did not have Dickens's
eye, which was ceaselessly searching for the telling gesture and detail.

The use Dostoevsky made of Edith (who, unlike her mother, is not
conceived in a Jonsonian mode) had more lasting consequences. Zina
Moskaleva, in her relations with her mother, is very like Edith. Consider the scene where Maria Aleksandrovna first broaches the subject
of marriage:

'Why all these twistings about, mother, when you can say it in
two words?' Zina said irately.
'Twistings about, Zina. Twistings about! And you can say such a
thing to your mother? But what am I!...'
'Enough, mother! Shall we quarrel over a word? Don't we
understand one another? Surely we have had time enough?'

Likewise Edith says: 'It is surely not worthwhile, Mama ... to observe
these forms of speech. We are quite alone. We know each other.'
Zina sings for the Prince, just as Edith plays the piano at Mr Dombey's
bidding. After the Prince's proposal, Zina announces that she will not
take on any further roles to entrap the Prince. Edith hates herself for
falling so low; she exhibits her accomplishments, but will not 'vaunt
or press the bargain'. And when the scandal breaks, Zina announces
that she is soiled and forever shamed. Zina's marriage is a 'bargain or
purchase', as of course is Edith's. The most obscure part of Edith
concerns her reasons for her marriage. Dostoevsky seems to be trying
to explain how anyone could enter into her situation. He was deaf to
Dickens's hints that her treatment by Mrs Skewton and Mr Dombey
amounted to violation. His solution is to increase the skill of the mother:
Maria Aleksandrovna persuades her daughter that it is the only way

out for her; that she will be doing the Prince a good turn; that in any case he will soon die; and that she will be able to give the school-teacher the care he needs, save his life and marry him. All this is rather weak, and in fact rather less interesting than the motives that can be discerned behind Edith's flights of rhetoric (as will be seen in the next chapter). But Zina has many of Edith's essentials: her wish to escape from an intolerable situation in society (it is not just financial pressure, as with Varvara Dobroselova and Dunia Raskolnikova); her sense of corruption; her consenting to sell herself in marriage; her queenly stance; her beauty; her pride. And perhaps Zina does end up as the masochist Edith is all along from the moment she first appears. In the last glimpse we have of Zina, she is married to a rich and important general and lives proud and inaccessible.[9]

The Uncle's Dream is the first striking evidence that the vividness of Dickens's dialogue and characterization was an important factor in Dostoevsky's response. Part of this can be put down to the higher standard of translation that now prevailed; Vvedensky's versions of Dombey, Pickwick, and Copperfield were particularly famous (and two or three different versions of each novel were generally available).[10] As yet, however, Dickens's influence was not assimilated; the more interesting influences for us are those in which Dostoevsky brought the results of his own experience and reflection to bear on his reading. In the 1850s he did not have the necessary knowledge to make an interesting character of Edith Dombey (he did not know anything about daemonic women). But the new characters introduced into this tale reappear in later works. Prince K. re-emerges as old Prince Sokolsky in Raw Youth, and Maria Aleksandrovna as Madame Stavrogina in The Devils (neither of these later characters has anything much of Mrs Skewton left in their make-up). And Zina–Edith, I will argue in the next chapter, reappears as Nastasia Filippovna in The Idiot, where metaphorical violation turns into actual rape.

In The Uncle's Dream Dostoevsky temporarily ceased to exist as a social writer and produced a rather unhumorous sketch of domestic life. Yet even before his prison sentence and exile he had been making efforts to move beyond his achievement in Poor Folk. His first attempt at a large novel had been Netochka Nezvanova; owing to his arrest in April 1849, it remained uncompleted, and only the first three parts were published. In the first section we see Netochka's life in a garret with her mother and stepfather, a musician of genius, who has turned to drink. Netochka's feelings for him are 'almost maternal'; she dreams of running away with him, and her wish is fulfilled after her mother dies. But the stepfather promptly abandons Netochka, who collapses on the pavement, from which by chance she is rescued by Prince Kh., a former benefactor of her father's. She begins life in a new household, where she develops a passionate love-hate relationship with the Prince's daughter. To protect the girls, they are separated and Netochka is entrusted to the care of the Prince's stepdaughter, Aleksandra Mikhailovna.

Futrell and Katarsky have found some good parallels between Netochka's life and adventures and those of Little Nell, Oliver Twist, and Florence Dombey. The similarities indicate that Dostoevsky responded to Dickens's child-figures, although it is striking that Dostoevsky understood several years before Dickens in what unhealthy ways a child's emotions might be manifested when they lacked natural outlets (the story of Netochka's friendship with the Prince's daughter is an anticipation of Miss Wade's Confession). It is, however, in the last section that certain other connections with *Dombey* (translated in 1847–8) are particularly suggestive. Aleksandra Mikhailovna, who takes charge of Netochka, was also raised in the Prince's household as a member of his family. Since her own father (an *otkupshchik*) had been engaged in trade, and since moreover, she did not have a large dowry, she could not hope to make a brilliant match, and so she was married off to a rich man with a good position in the bureaucracy (there is something here of the complexity – but little of the interest – of Mr Dombey's and the Hon. Mrs Granger's respective positions in society). In her new family Netochka is placed, like Florence, between a cold father and a loving mother. At the same time she is troubled about the relationship between her new parents. Petr Aleksandrovich has some sort of secret power over his wife, who always feels constrained in his presence. One day Netochka learns the reason for the mystery from a letter she chances to find in a book (*St Ronan's Well*). Sometime after her marriage Aleksandra Mikhailovna had fallen in love. The affair remained an innocent one, yet her husband has never really forgiven her, and continually flaunts his moral superiority. He even enjoys making her suffer; once Netochka catches him suppressing a smile and putting on a countenance of moral rectitude in front of a mirror. There are a series of 'grim, dark scenes' between husband and wife. In one of these Aleksandra Mikhailovna stands 'supporting herself against the mantelpiece', and the position of her body expresses 'unbearable torture' (a reminiscence surely of the Edith who strikes her hand on a marble shelf, and then sits by the fire, watching the 'shapes of outrage and affront' flickering on the wall in *Dombey*, ch. 42). Netochka (like Florence) becomes an added source of tension. In the last of the scenes (at which point the novel is broken off), Aleksandra Mikhailovna accuses her husband of wanting to destroy all capacity for natural feeling in Netochka and herself.[11]

The theme of the unhappily married woman is characteristic of George Sand. But because of the role of Netochka, it is possible that *Dombey* was the influence leading Dostoevsky to extend his social range. In this novel Dickens's view of marriage and children in relation to society attained new levels of seriousness (and, at times, of melodramatic effect). If we imagine that Dostoevsky was using the basic scheme he had found in *Dombey*, we can see that certain modifications would have been necessary. Netochka could not have been entrusted by the kind and understanding Prince to so tormented and unstable a couple as the Dombeys, and Edith could not have helped Netochka to escape from the fantastic, self-enclosed world of her childhood. But allowing for this, the equivalent Dostoevsky gives us for the conflict and hostility in Dickens's novel is clumsy and inadequate. Mr Dombey's pride of possession and atrophied feeling turn into a relatively crude combination of cruelty and self-righteousness; there is too much of the conventional villain in Petr Aleksandrovich. It is true that there is something mysterious about the relationship between Edith and Dombey; it seems to have greater significance than is in fact achieved. Nevertheless, Dostoevsky's own ability to use new types and themes did not come all at once. His imagination at this stage was very much an adolescent's; he understood introspective types, dreamers, and romantic lovers, and had a special insight into delusions threatening a person's sense of identity. Outside this range he tended to fall back on conventional characters and explanations.

If *Netochka Nezvanova* is seen in relation to the theme of community, there is a little more to be said. L. P. Grossman has retrieved a remark that Netochka originally made, but which Dostoevsky later discarded:[12]

My life in a strange family had left too strong a mark on the first impressions of my heart, and accordingly the sense of family

[*chuvstvo semeistvennosti*] so poeticized in the novels of Walter Scott
– that feeling in whose name they were written, a feeling raised
to the highest historical significance, presented as a condition for
the preservation of all mankind, and so lovingly brought forth
in all his novels – pressed into my heart too sweetly, too
strongly, in response to my memories and my own longings.

Considering the way Dostoevsky subsequently coupled the names of
Scott and Dickens, and considering, too, Dickens's celebration of
family life coupled with his pervasive sense of the breakdown of the
family, we can wonder whether Dickens possibly led Dostoevsky to
the problem of the random or accidental family which emerges in his
later novels. The existing injustice in society, and the weakness and
evil in man were large obstacles to the creation of a community; the
collapse of the family – the institution in which the notion of community was rooted – made the ideal even more remote.

In *The Insulted and the Injured* (1861) Dostoevsky is still in the grip of
the ideals and searchings of his pre-Siberian years. This work is, however, pervaded by a new cynicism about social brotherhood and about
the Schilleresque ideals of noble passion and sacrifice. Dickens's influence in this novel has long been recognized in the case of Nellie
and suspected in the case of the villain, Prince Valkovsky.[13] These
figures are worth brief consideration for what they show about the
disintegration of the old ideal of community and about Dostoevsky's
need to develop a structure into which monsters of vice and virtue
could be incorporated. Nellie's relationship with the angel-figure at
the heart of *The Old Curiosity Shop* is at once apparent (she is even
half-English). Some of Dostoevsky's phrasing is taken directly from
Dickens. The narrator, Vania says (pt. II, ch. 11): 'And he let you!
Nellie! Nellie!' The grandfather in Dickens's novel exclaims (ch. 1):
'I don't consider her! ah, how little you know the truth! little Nelly,
little Nelly!' Both the Nellies want to be independent of other men,
except for what they can get by begging. But Dostoevsky's heroine
has been exposed to a much harsher world. Her mother had run off
with a ruthless and selfish aristocrat (Prince Valkovsky), taking with
her part of her father's fortune. Soon afterwards she was abandoned,
yet though she was left destitute her father, old Smith, refused ever to
forgive her. But eventually the old man made friends with Nellie,
the child born of the union. By this time he himself had nothing left,

and to provide for him, Nellie turned to begging. His nature was so suspicious that he would seize the alms from her the moment she received them (Little Nell's grandfather stole from her, but only because of his uncontrollable passion for gambling). Because Dostoevsky is a faithful psychologist, his heroine is marked by her experience; she is embittered and suspicious. She does not like accepting Vania's kindness without repaying him in some way (and this she is able to do very effectively at first, by caring for him during his illness, in a scene deriving from the Marchioness and Dick Swiveller). Under the stress of her memories and of what she hears of Natasha Ikhmeneva, whose mother had cursed her for her relationship with Prince Valkovsky's son, Nellie even tries to run away; there is a horrifying glimpse of her begging on a bridge. The narrator observes that she seems to 'enjoy her pain', and speaks of a sort of 'egoism of suffering' to be found among the poor and oppressed.

There is little need for demonstrating Nellie's greater psychological complexity, but perhaps we can find some pointers as to why Dostoevsky admired Little Nell. His own heroine retains Nell's lovingness and innocence as an ideal, and if she is a rebel, it is only because of the evil she found enshrined in society. Whereas Little Nell can redeem a whole society by her death, Nellie is instrumental in reconciling Natasha with her father. At Vania's instigation, she tells old Ikhmenev the whole story of her own and her mother's sufferings, and the obstinate old man is so agitated that he is on the point of running out to look for his daughter (who has been abandoned by her lover) when the door opens and Natasha rushes in, pale and dishevelled, her clothes soaked with rain, to be reunited to him. Soon after Nellie dies in a room filled with flowers in the midst of her adoring friends (Nell dies in winter, and so her bed is covered with leaves and winter berries). Nellie is a figure symbolizing man's need for the ideal; when she imagines she cannot find it in society, she escapes; but she can help to reconcile mankind. Even if social brotherhood was remote, a figure like Nellie could keep man's aspiration for it alive. And surely Dickens's heroine had something of the same significance for Dostoevsky.

The figure set against Nellie is Prince Valkovsky. Here Dostoevsky deals explicitly with the problem of evil. Previously his vicious characters hurt people more or less unconsciously (if we leave out of account the magician Murin in *The Landlady*, along with the uninteresting Petr Aleksandrovich in *Netochka* and the autobiographical *House of the*

Dead). Valkovsky deliberately establishes his power over men and mocks their ideals. With his refined yet brutal sensuality, he has affinities with the heroes of sadistic fiction. Because of his persecution of good, his intrigues, and his open pursuit of self-interest, there have been various attempts to relate him to Dickens's villains, in particular Ralph Nickleby and Quilp. There is, surely, good reason for these connections: the role of Dickens's sentimental heroes and heroines is so closely bound up with their persecutors that it is natural to suppose that Valkovsky's role, no less than Nellie's, derives from Dickens. But the connections with Ralph and Quilp can be drawn only in rather general terms. In one scene there are signs of a more specific influence (which is later at work in *The Devils* as well). The Prince has insisted on stopping at a restaurant with Vania, and there reveals his intention of breaking off his son's entanglement with Nastasia, in order to marry him to Katia, whose fortune Valkovsky is anxious to get hold of. Valkovsky affects to speak in a tone of casual friendship, and is drinking champagne, which he repeatedly offers to Vania. Although Vania is repelled by the man and refuses to drink with him, he is forced to sit and listen. Mr (or Sir John) Chester in *Barnaby Rudge* is a man with a similar past and motives (and also with a mask-like face). Both men come from aristocratic families, and being impoverished, have married for money. Both have a child (Hugh, Nellie) whom they do not acknowledge, and neglect and persecute. Chester schemes to prevent his son Edward's marriage to Emma Haredale, the niece of an old enemy (Ikhmenev too has become an enemy of Valkovsky), and wants him to make a suitable marriage in order to repair the family fortunes. And there is a scene in which Chester, with his perfect ease of manner, reveals his plots to Mr Haredale while entreating him to share in the enjoyment of some wine.[14]

Dostoevsky's novel is an ambiguous one. Prince Valkovsky succeeds in his designs, yet thanks to Nellie the Ikhmenevs and Vania manage to turn evil into good, and reassert the power of forgiveness and brotherhood. The novel ends on a seemingly happy note; Nastasia realizes that her love for Alesha Valkovsky was a sort of delirium, from which she has recovered, and when Vania looks into her eyes, they appear to say: 'We could be forever happy together' (*my by mogli byt' naveki schastlivy vmeste*). But, as the narrator, Vania, has told us at the outset, the novel is an account of his life some months ago, and he is writing it as he lies in hospital with little hope of recovery. Clearly this is an allusion to the catastrophe which struck Dostoevsky when he was arrested and sentenced to Siberia. *The Insulted and Injured* dramatizes Dostoevsky's uncertainty about his ideals of the Forties and about his own situation in life. There is an ambiguity about the power of evil in the world, a suggestion that social brotherhood is little more than a dream. But the novel is not a convincing one. There is something gratuitous about Valkovsky's wickedness; the difficulty is not so much that it is unmotivated or even that Dostoevsky's wish to connect it with an atheistic outlook is too facile. If we contrast Valkovsky with those later figures of evil, Svidrigailov and Stavrogin, we might wonder whether even a great Dostoevskian villain is a source of significance in himself, or whether he does not receive his importance from the larger structure of which he is part.

Dostoevsky's difficulties in the late Fifties and Sixties were not only those of a man freed from a long ordeal, or of an ambitious writer whose career had been interrupted at a crucial moment. He had been isolated for too long from the discussions animating his fellow intellectuals, and in Siberia he had no real opportunity of seeing what was happening to Russia. *Notes from the Underground* in 1864 and *Crime and Punishment* in 1866 were the first works in which the promise of genius in Dostoevsky's earliest writings was at last fulfilled. His range and perspective were very different now; he was concerned with ideology, with socialism, political economy, and the meaning of the Christian message; he was aware of his country and the changes taking place in it; and as he lived in and observed society, he was able to ponder and draw on the knowledge and experience he had acquired in the convict-prison and in his relations with Apollinaria Suslova.

Notes

1 *Stat'i*, pp. 11f.
2 'A Weak Heart', pp. 526, 548 (in *Sobranie socheninii*, vol. 1).
3 *Chuzzlewit*, ch. 2, pp. 17, 22; ch. 12, p. 194. Other similarities: Vasia stands outside Liza's door, listening to her play the piano, and Tom listens to Mary playing his organ; Arkady with his well-meaning but somewhat boorish insensitivity lies somewhere between young Martin and John Westlock.
4 'A Weak Heart', pp. 546, 550; *Chuzzlewit*, ch. 53, p. 823.
5 *Sobranie sochinenii*, vol. 2, p. 582.
6 *Chuzzlewit*, ch. 20, p. 329; ch. 30, pp. 476, 484. Note too: Iulian Mastakovich catches sight of himself in a mirror looking red as a lobster, and Pecksniff looks at himself in the parson's little mirror.

7 *Dikkens v Rossii* (Moscow, 1966), pp. 373f.

8 *Dombey*, ch. 27, p. 384; *The Uncle's Dream*, ch. 8, p. 337 (in *Sobranie sochinenii*, vol. 2).

9 *The Uncle's Dream*, ch. 5, pp. 305f., 314; ch. 8, p. 337; ch. 9, p. 354; ch. 14, p. 394. *Dombey*, ch. 26, p. 373; ch. 27, pp. 392, 395.

10 Vvedensky's declaration to Dickens, 'From the banks of the Neva to the remotest parts of Siberia you are read with avidity', was more significant than he suspected.

11 *Netochka*, ch. 6, pp. 176ff.; ch. 7, 194–201, 210, 214, 229f. (in *Sobranie sochinenii*, vol. 2).

12 Vol. 22, pp. 73f. in the 'Prosveshchenie' edition of Dostoevsky's works.

13 The fullest and most recent discussion is in Katarsky, pp. 389–99.

14 *The Insulted and Injured*, pt. III, ch. 10; *Barnaby Rudge*, ch. 12.

4

The Idiot:
melodrama and ideal

Melodramatic machinery

Dostoevsky set to work on *The Idiot* shortly after arriving in Geneva in August 1867. The idea shaping his imagination was change. The main group of characters in the first plans[1] was a family of decayed and impoverished landowners who had wound up in St Petersburg; in contrast to them was the Uncle, who from being cast on to the streets as a young man had grown into a rich and successful money-lender. It was a world – evocative of Dickens's – of warped family relationships and unhealthy feelings. In the principal family, Handsome had the role of favourite, while his younger brother – the Idiot – and a foster-child, Mignon, were exploited and mistreated (Mignon, it appears, was associated in Dostoevsky's mind with the character of this name in *Wilhelm Meister* and with Olga Umetskaia, a girl who came before the courts in September 1867 because she had tried to burn down her parents' home in retaliation for their brutal treatment of her). Mignon dreamed of revenge, while the Idiot, a man of violent passions, attempted to dominate himself out of pride (p. 16) and an inordinate ego (p. 21). The Uncle had turned proud and suspicious as a result of his experiences, and was afraid to love people (p. 13). The Heroine, on whom the plot centred, was another proud character, original, capricious, superior to her environment, and of a poetical nature (p. 21). Her family wanted to 'sell her off' (p. 17), and by way of revenge, she was playing off her suitors – Handsome, the Idiot, the Uncle's son – against one another.

For three months Dostoevsky struggled with these characters, transforming them, switching them from one family group to another, introducing new figures, and trying out marriages and affairs in different combinations. As plan succeeded plan, the name of Mignon gave way to Umetskaia and the motif of rape became associated with her; she acquired two doubles, Ustinia and Nastia (pp. 82ff.); the Idiot suddenly turned into a Prince (p. 76); attempts were made to save this proud young man (e.g. pp. 28, 41). But Dostoevsky could not find a basic story or situation, a framework round which his imagination could work (the Russian word for plot used by him, *fabula*, is suggestive). Finally, on 4 December (N.S.), with his deadline fast approaching (the first instalment of his novel had to appear in the January number of *Russkii vestnik*), he scrapped his preliminary notes and worked furiously on a new outline. On the eighteenth he began writing; on 5 January he sent off the first five chapters, and on the eleventh another two. In a letter written two days later, he explained to his niece, Sonia Ivanova, what it was that had released his creative powers:

> The idea of the novel is an old and precious one of mine, but so difficult that for long I have not dared to attempt it; and if I have decided to attempt it now, it is only because I found myself in an almost desperate situation. The chief idea of the novel is to depict a positively beautiful [*polozhitel'no prekrasnyi*] man. There is nothing more difficult in the world, especially nowadays. All writers – not only our own but even all the European ones – who have attempted to depict the *positively* [Dostoevsky's italics] beautiful have always missed. For it is a measureless task. The beautiful is an [the] ideal, and neither our ideal, nor civilized Europe's is close to being worked out. There is only one positively beautiful person in the world – Christ – and the appearance of this measurelessly, infinitely beautiful person is, of course, an infinite miracle. (The whole Gospel of John is conceived in this way: the whole miracle is seen just in the incarnation, just in the appearance of the beautiful.) But I've wandered too far. I'll simply say that of the beautiful persons in Christian literature the most perfect is Don Quixote. But he is beautiful only because at the same time he is funny [*smeshon*]. Dickens's Pickwick (an infinitely weaker idea than Don Quixote, but all the same immense) is also funny, and succeeds only because of this. Compassion arises for the beautiful when it is laughed at and ignorant of its own worth – and so sympathy arises in the reader. This rousing of compassion is the secret of humour.

Jean Valjean is also a strong attempt, but he arouses sympathy
because of his terrible misfortune and the injustice of society to
him. I have nothing of the kind, nothing at all, and therefore
I am terribly afraid it will be a positive failure. (no. 294, *Pis'ma*,
vol. 2)

Pickwick helped Dostoevsky to define his new conception of the
Idiot, and appeared to him as an attempt to portray the Christian ideal.
What Dostoevsky's reasons were, and whether his own view of the
ideal bore some relation to that held by 'civilized Europe', are
questions to consider. But the discussion is, I think, more illuminating
if certain questions concerning Prince Myshkin's relationship with
Natsasia Filippovna are taken up first. There is the more justification
for this as Nastasia probably played a bigger part than Myshkin in
shaping the novel. In the letter of 12 January to A. N. Maikov (no. 292,
Pis'ma, vol. 2), Dostoevsky said:

On the whole there is a plan. Details are glimmering ahead,
alluring me and keeping up my ardour. But the whole? the hero?
Because the whole is emerging under the guise of the *hero*.
That's how it has worked out. I have to set down an image.
Will it develop as I write? And imagine what horrors have
happened just like that: besides the hero, it has turned out there
is a heroine, so that there are TWO HEROES!! And besides these
heroes there are two absolutely major characters, that is to say,
near-heroes. (As for accessory characters – of whom a long account
will be required – there is a countless multitude and the novel is
in 8 parts.) Of the four heroes – two are firmly outlined *in my
soul*; one still isn't outlined at all; and the fourth, i.e. the principal,
i.e. first hero, is extremely weak. Maybe he is not lodged weakly
in my heart – but he is extremely difficult.

To begin, let us accept Dostoevsky's own description of his hero
as an attempt to set forth the Christian ideal. The society into which
Dostoevsky introduces him is such as to make any effective action
impossible. It is a hot-house in which unnatural passions – and above
all a lust for money – are bred. Investment and speculation are the chief
social mechanism; they have made General Epanchin a distinguished
personage, and engage the energies of Lebedev and Ptitsyn. Gania
Ivolgin – the representative ordinary man – will do anything for money.

Love, marriage, honour – are commodities. The corruption of values is flagrantly displayed in the attitudes men take towards Nastasia Filippovna. Totsky has offered his former mistress a dowry of seventy-five thousand roubles by way of compensation and in the hope of marrying her off. Gania wants to take her, thinking that with the dowry he can restore his family's good name. Rogozhin believes he can purchase her love by bidding a hundred thousand roubles. But – and here lurks a problem – it could be argued that the general corruption of society is reflected even in the Prince's offer of marriage. In the big, public scene in which Nastasia's fate is decided, he can intervene only by offering himself as a husband. Given her feelings of victimization and the division in her nature, torn as it is between desire and a lost dream of chastity and wholeness, marriage to a perfectly compassionate man would surely be as intolerable for her as Rogozhin's all-possessive love. We are more aware of what this union would signify (forgiveness and acceptance of forgiveness) than of what it could *be*. In proposing to substitute a marriage based on compassion for a marriage based on money or lust, it looks as though the Prince is introducing a false relationship of his own. The Prince's failure seems to be one of understanding rather than of compassion, and it would be hard to accept the necessity for this sort of separation between mind and wisdom of the heart unless we felt the Prince really had no other possibility of action.

According to this line of argument, it follows that Dostoevsky in some sense failed to portray the ideal man. Or perhaps this particular action of the Prince was a mistake: if we take Dostoevsky's model of the ideal, Christ, we see that the nature of his mission only gradually becomes clear (even to himself, especially in the Gospel of St John), although of course we can at no stage imagine him compromising in Myshkin's way with the values of the world. The Prince's offer in the public-auction scene might have been a mistake leading to greater self-knowledge. Dostoevsky himself partly countenances such an interpretation. Myshkin is aware, from an early stage, that his love for Nastasia Filippovna is compassionate in its basis, and when he falls in love with Aglaia he begins to realize his compassionate love is a threat to his new, previously unknown (but still unsensual) emotion. Yet can it be said that the novel is mainly about Myshkin's *discovery* of his own inadequacy and failure? He has, to be sure, a sense of inadequacy and failure, but while this sense brings about his ultimate collapse, it never causes him to re-examine his actions and priorities. It never even gives him a sense of the impossibility of action, and simply leads him into greater and greater confusion.

It may be prejudging the issue to assume that the ideal man must be capable of effective action, or even that Dostoevsky's hero does in fact correspond to his intentions. Without going into these matters here, suppose we take at its face-value Nastasia Filippovna's statement that Myshkin's proposal is a revelation of kindness, goodness, and honesty such as for years she has been awaiting. In the scene of the public auction, Nastasia Filippovna's innermost ideal is laid bare, and at the same time she realizes that the hero of her dreams can only be a child, and would be destroyed if she married him. But if the elaborate scene of the public auction is set up to reveal her private ideal, there arises with particular urgency the question of what her significance is, and why her extravagant behaviour should be the subject of such interest. Why does Dostoevsky build up his novel round her?

Suppose, however, that Myshkin's proposal is seen not just as a revelation of a private ideal but as a comment on the attitudes and behaviour of men in his society. Then, while the Prince's qualities may be desirable (or not) in themselves, the relative importance we attach to them will to some extent depend on whether we feel Dostoevsky has given us a true picture of Russian society. And here doubts must arise. Because of the violence of the incidents, and because of the basic simplicity and starkness of the choices confronting Nastasia Filippovna, the marriage auction looks very much like melodrama. She is, in effect, being asked to choose between sensual passion and compassionate love – hardly, as it stands, a meaningful alternative. There is nothing Dostoevsky liked so much as a public scandal stretching over several chapters, and it is possible he was simply carried away by the theatrical possibilities of the situation, as he himself feared (see Letter no. 301, *Pis'ma*, vol. 2). Certainly, it is difficult not to be aware of the manipulation required to set up the scene. The Prince has to arrive at the height of Nastasia Filippovna's name-day party. He first meets her in the afternoon at the Ivolgins', by which time he knows everything there is to know about her, and Dostoevsky has to fill in the interval between this encounter and the party in the evening, which he does very entertainingly by sending the Prince on one of General Ivolgin's drunken peregrinations (in pt. I, ch. 12). But for all the genius with which it is handled the episode is a bridge-device; it has nothing to do with the main plot, and cannot stop us wondering why, say, Myshkin did not try to speak to Nastasia Filippovna in private, before the public gathering. Thus, once again, we come up against the question to which all the other questions lead: why is there the exciting melodrama of the public marriage auction? This is a question about Dostoevsky's artistry and also, I suggest, a question about the origin of the scene.

Nastasia Filippovna and Edith Dombey

In the early plans of *The Idiot* Dostoevsky was obsessed with the theme of pride, and in the context of the bare character sketches he draws, it is particularly easy to remember that this was an obsession Dickens shared with him; Estella, Lady Dedlock, Mrs Clennam, Mr Dorrit, Miss Wade, were all, in their different ways, studies of pride, as was the whole of *Dombey and Son*. Here and there in the notebooks we may recognize potential Dickensian characters (especially the Heroine and the Uncle), although the descriptions are so brief that it would be dangerous to build very much on to them. But because of Dostoevsky's interest in pride (it is, of course, an important theme throughout his literary work), the suggestion to be made here, that Edith Dombey was an important formative influence on Nastasia Filippovna, may seem the less surprising. The characters in the notebooks that eventually turn into the Nastasia Filippovna of the novel are, as P. N. Sakulin has shown, Mignon–Umetskaia and Nastia, along with the Heroine (who is also related to Aglaia). In them her desire for revenge and her sense of defilement can be found, and so too can her pride and her oscillations between suitors. Whether or not these projected characters had Dickensian sources or associations (the Heroine, with her sadistic treatment of the prototype Idiot, sounds rather like Estella), Nastasia Filippovna has several important characteristics which are not all recognizably present in the notebooks, and which suggest that she took shape in Dostoevsky's mind under the influence, conscious or not, of Edith Dombey.

Both characters represent a familiar group from the world of melodrama. The one is presented to us as a kept woman (although it is soon made clear she is no ordinary cocotte); and the other, we are given with much indirection to understand, is the moral equivalent of a kept woman or prostitute. Both, of course, are very beautiful, and both very proud. About their beauty there is something mysterious. Of Edith we are told: 'It was a remarkable characteristic of this lady's beauty that it appeared to vaunt and assert itself without her aid, and against her will. She knew that she was beautiful: it was impossible that it could be otherwise: but she seemed with her own pride to defy her very self.' Dickens is teasing our curiosity here, and eventually offers this for an explanation:[2]

> 'I have dreamed,' said Edith in a low voice, 'of a pride that is all powerless for good, all powerful for evil; of a pride that has been galled and goaded, through many shameful years, and has never recoiled except upon itself; a pride that has debased its owner with the consciousness of deep humiliation, and never helped its owner boldly to resent it or avoid it, or to say, "This shall not be!" a pride that, rightly guided, might have led perhaps to better things, but which, misdirected and perverted, like all else belonging to the same possessor, has been self-contempt, mere hardihood, and ruin.'
>   She neither looked nor spoke to Florence now, but went on as if she were alone.
>   'I have dreamed,' she said, 'of such indifference and callousness, arising from this self-contempt; this wretched, inefficient, miserable pride; that it has gone on with listless steps even to the altar, yielding to the old, familiar, beckoning finger, – oh mother, oh mother! – while it spurned it; and willing to be hateful to itself for once and for all, rather than to be stung daily in some new form. Mean, poor thing!'

We have not much taste for this rhetoric nowadays, but it might be overhasty to dismiss this as a mere juggling with moral counters emptied of all meaning. For behind Edith Dombey a very interesting woman can be recognized, a woman not unlike the Nastasia Filippovna seen by Prince Myshkin:[3]

> 'This unhappy woman is deeply convinced that she is the most fallen, most vicious of beings on earth. Oh, do not shame her, don't cast a stone. She has tortured herself too much with the consciousness of her own undeserved shame! And of what is she guilty, oh God! Oh every minute she cries out in a frenzy that she doesn't admit to any guilt, that she's the victim of others,

the victim of a dissolute and wicked man; but whatever she says
to you – she is, you must know, the first not to believe it. With
all her conscience she believes, on the contrary, that she is herself –
guilty. When I tried to dispel that darkness, she would be driven
into such sufferings that my heart can never heal as long as
I remember that awful time. It is as if my heart was pierced once
and for all. She ran away from me, you know what for? – just to
show me that she was low. But the most awful thing of all is
that she herself, maybe, did not know she only wanted to prove
this to me, and ran away because she felt inwardly pressed to do a
shameful deed, so that she could say to herself then and there:
"Look at your new shame – you are a low creature!" . . . Do you
know, in this continuous consciousness of her shame, there is
perhaps a kind of awful, unnatural pleasure for her, a sort of
revenge on someone. Sometimes, I could make her almost see
light round her again, but straight away she would again rebel
and go so far as bitterly to accuse me of setting myself above her
(when I had no thought of it), and in the end she declared to me
when I wanted to marry her, that she did not need anybody's
overbearing compassion, nor anybody's help, nor anybody "to
raise her up". You saw her yesterday; do you think she is happy
in that company, that that is her society?'

Nastasia Filippovna's whole outlook has been determined by the rape
committed on her when she was sixteen. Everything she experiences
after this has served only to confirm her sense of the impurity infecting
herself and the whole world. Nobody belonging to the same society
as her guardian, who corrupted her, has the right to say anything
about love, family life, forgiveness, or happiness. Although she can
look to the friendship of humble school-teachers and laundry-women,
it has no very deep meaning for her. There are two realities for her –
one where she is wicked and corrupt (Rogozhin's), and a dream-world
of childlike innocence and purity (Prince Myshkin's). But when the
Prince appears to her, she finds that, in fact, he can offer her nothing.
Looking at her from the outside without really entering into her situation, we might want to say, along with Aglaia and Evgeny Pavlovich
Radomsky,[4] that Nastasia Filippovna's behaviour shows excessive
pride and self-love, as though nothing could ever be good enough for
her.

There is a point of contact here with Edith Dombey's self-lacerating pride, of which Dickens took very much the external view. Can it be said, though, that Edith Dombey was a formative influence on Nastasia Filippovna? It may be worth listing some other parallels between the two women, before returning to the question of masochistic pride. Edith's soul 'recoils' from Dombey; she feels 'aversion and contempt' for him in place of love. Similarly, Nastasia Filippovna has had nothing but 'contempt, nauseous contempt' for Totsky.[5] (Dombey is both violator and marriage-partner, abetted in both roles by Mrs Skewton; Dostoevsky separates the themes, with a consequent gain in clarity.) Edith scorns Dombey's money, but demands it 'as her right, her bargain – as the base and worthless recompense for which she had become his wife'. Nastasia accepts Totsky's seventy-five thousand roubles 'not as payment for her degradation as a young girl, for which she was not responsible, but simply as a recompense for her perverted fate', and has lived in the luxury he offered to her, without attaching any real importance to it.[6] In the end Nastasia and Edith abandon everything they have received. Nastasia Filippovna is 'demoniac', and her soul is filled with 'darkness', while Edith is possessed, at any rate on one occasion, by a legion of devils, and her beauty and her eyes are continually darkened.[7] When Edith is possessed, her eyes seem to sparkle fire – another attribute she shares with Nastasia Filippovna.[8] Indeed, fire is an element to which they have a strong attraction: Edith sits 'enthroned upon a couch by the fire' (ch. 45); she holds her hand near the fire as if to burn it (ch. 42); in Dijon she sits waiting for Carker in a small room filled with clusters of burning candles, which has to be reached through a succession of large, dark rooms (ch. 54). Nastasia Filippovna draws on the powers of fire to enact her revenge on society when she tosses the packet of one hundred thousand roubles on to the fire, and challenges Gania to pick it out. Both women are murderous, yet both have an angelic as well as a demoniac side to their natures (and inevitably they are viewed – but with rather different effect – as 'fallen angels'). The Edith that Florence knows is quite unlike the Edith seen by anyone else (ch. 30, p. 422): 'how different this lady's beauty was, from what she had supposed . . . her manner was so subdued and gentle, that if she had been of Florence's own age and character, it scarcely could have invited confidence more.' Similarly, Prince Myshkin sees something childlike in Nastasia Filippovna's face when he studies her photograph (pt. I, ch. 7, p. 92): 'This face, unusual for its beauty as well as for something else, now struck him even more strongly. It was as though there was boundless pride and contempt, almost hatred, in this face, and at the same time something astonishingly simple-hearted [*chto-to udivitel'no prostodushnoe*].' Edith looks to Florence for comfort, just as Nastasia looks to her heaven-sent Prince. Both of them wish to make sacrifices for these embodiments of their better selves, and are incapable of doing so. And under the strain of their split personalities, both of them are going mad.[9]

What yields the most convincing evidence that Edith was an influence on Nastasia – and points to some of the outstanding differences between them – lies in the terms in which their marriages are conceived. For Edith everything she does is part of a 'sordid and miserable transaction'; she has been 'hawked and vended here and there' (ch. 27, pp. 391, 394). When her mother chides her for not offering more encouragement to Mr Dombey, she answers, 'raising her head and trembling in her energy of shame and pride':

'No! Who takes me, refuse that I am, and as I well deserve to be . . . shall take me, as this man does, with no art of mine put forth to lure him. He sees me at the auction, and he thinks it well to buy me. Let him! When he came to view me – perhaps to bid – he required to see the roll of my accomplishments. I gave it to him. When he would have me show one of them, to justify his purchase to his men, I require of him to say which he demands, and I exhibit it. I will do no more. He makes the purchase of his own will, and with his own sense of its worth, and the power of his money; and I hope it may never disappoint him. I have not vaunted and pressed the bargain; neither have you, so far as I have been able to prevent you.' (ch. 27, p. 395)

Edith is in the marriage-market, as her rhetorical speech informs us. But the auction remains a metaphor; the forms of courtship and marriage are observed. What Dostoevsky does is to take the idea of the marriage auction and dramatize it. If marriage can only be a sordid bargain for Nastasia Filippovna, then he will have a real auction, not just a figurative one, and show all the bidders and their motives. On the one hand, there is Gania Ivolgin, who is in the bidding with the backing of Totsky's seventy-five thousand roubles; on the other – the merchant, Rogozhin, who bids one hundred thousand. And against them both is the Prince, who bids Pure Love, backed with a little personal fortune he has just come into. We see here Dostoevsky's tendency to give dramatic expression to his themes; indeed the marriage auction is so fully dramatized that it impinges on all the characters present in ever shifting ways.

The important differences between Edith and Nastasia are due to a difference in method. Dickens had a peculiar genius as a moralist, a genius akin to Hogarth's, as F. R. Leavis[10] has reminded us. In a moral picture like the following there is a vivid and complex realization of Edith Dombey's situation:

> Slowly and thoughtfully did Edith wander alone through the mansion of which she was so soon to be the lady; and little heed took she of all the elegance and splendour it began to display. The same indomitable haughtiness of soul, the same proud scorn expressed in eye and lip, the same fierce beauty, only tamed by a sense of its own little worth, and of the little worth of everything around it, went through the grand saloons and halls that had got loose among the shady trees, and raged and rent themselves. The mimic roses on the walls and floors were set round with sharp thorns, that tore her breast; in every scrap of gold so dazzling to the eye, she saw some hateful atom of her purchase-money; the broad high mirrors showed her, at full length, a woman with a noble quality yet dwelling in her nature, who was too false to her better self, and too debased and lost, to save herself. She believed that all this was so plain, more or less, to all eyes, that she had no resource or power of self-assertion but in pride: and with this pride, which tortured her own heart night and day, she fought her fate out, braved it, and defied it. (ch. 30, p. 423)

The description is so rich in meanings which are not developed elsewhere that the words of G. H. Lewes about Dickens readily come to mind: 'He was a seer of visions . . . in no other perfectly sane mind . . . have I observed vividness of imagination approaching so closely to hallucination.'[11] The awareness embodied in this scene is closely bound up with the manner of seeing (the rooms of the household raging and renting themselves, the dazzling gold, the roses on the wallpaper tearing Edith's breast). Because of the intense, though metaphorical, realization of Edith's feelings, Dickens understands here that her pride is only an appearance. But when Edith moves away from the mirror in which her dilemma is reflected, he is at a considerable loss to explain her. With Dickens it is often as though he saw more than he could understand. Edith belongs with those 'gristly figures' who, Chesterton says, 'were keeping something back from the author as well as from the reader'.[12] Consider again the account Edith gives to Florence (see above, p. 57). This explanation is cast largely in terms of pride, yet there are aspects to Edith's problem – a sense of injury, of corruption, of inevitability about her choices – that the declamation abou pride (a moral rather than a psychological term) hardly begins to cover. The reference to her 'self-contempt' is much more promising, and Dickens seems to be groping towards a way of saying that her self-hatred is really a twisted form of self-love, but he was not sufficiently aware of what he was doing to see that the rest was melodrama. He can dramatize (or rather depict) a sudden insight into a situation, but since he lacks a vocabulary for discussing the psychological reasons for behaviour, he falls back on the rhetoric of a Wronged or Guilty Woman. The original vision is never altogether lost; Dickens renders her pride and her masochism through some effective stage-business, as when Edith presses her bracelet into her arm, or dashes her arm against the marble chimney-shelf.[13] But because of his failure to understand Edith's psychology, this basically dynamic character is not a success; for the most part (the beginning of the scene in chapter 40 is an exception) her quarrels with Dombey take the form of empty melodramatic collisions (yet the speech of Dickens's more static characters is memorable). For the same reason, Dickens fails to see that Edith should present more of a problem to morality; that there is, indeed, something strangely amoral about her behaviour.

The relationship between the two characters can now be stated. Dickens has the makings of an interesting character in Edith Dombey. In her he draws a connection between pride and masochism – a pride feeding on hatred of the self and of the world. He sees that pride can serve as a disguise for masochism, but not that masochism is itself a form of self-love. Because of her masochism Edith sells herself to Dombey, but can only hate herself and the marriage transaction. Dickens's methods enable him to show pride and masochism in their moral and physical aspect – but not to explain their psychological basis. Lacking a gift for the analysis of behaviour, he cannot really fit this character into the detailed working out of the plot, and she turns into a melodramatic heroine. With Nastasia Filippovna Dostoevsky makes use of both the themes of masochistic pride and the marriage auction, but handles them dramatically. At the same time, he is able to see, for instance, that Nastasia's masochism is really a form of self-love. It would appear that he is responding to Edith Dombey much more fully (but also far more distinctively) than in *The Uncle's Dream* or in *Netochka Nezvanova* (see above, chapter 3), in which the theme of masochism is hardly touched on (even Zina Moskaleva is little more than an unhappy, suffering woman) and the auction is an ordinary transaction. One reason for the difference probably has to do with Dostoevsky's own experience; his affair with Apollinaria Suslova had given him insight into a person's ability to inflict punishment on himself and on others. In *The Gambler* (1866) he drew on this knowledge to portray the tortured relations of Polina and Aleksei.[14] Under the immediate shock of De Grieux's abandonment (and possibly too of Aleksei's failure to understand why she has come to him) Polina insists on selling herself to Aleksei. But unlike Nastasia, she does not sell herself in marriage; the selling is not an auction; she is not incurably a masochist. And she is not a melodramatic creature. For Nastasia Filippovna, though she is a successful dramatic character, comes from the world of melodrama. She bears the marks of her origins in her position of a wronged and fallen woman; in her aspirations for purity; in her style of life. Like Edith she even uses rhetoric, but like Edith her rhetoric is addressed not so much at the reader, in an attempt to persuade him of her sense of wrong or of her fundamental nobility, as to herself and to the other characters who are the immediate audience of her quest for identity.

Enough has been said to suggest an answer to the question: why is there the exciting melodrama of the public auction in *The Idiot*? Dostoevsky was writing under the influence of that strange character, Edith Dombey, but was using his own distinctive methods in handling Dickens's themes. There remains the question of what the significance of the auction scene is – whether, so to speak, Nastasia Filippovna has run away with the story, or whether the scene is assimilated into the fabric of the novel. In *Dombey*, Dickens made the private lives of a small group of characters a vehicle of meaning about society as a whole. He wanted to show the self-defeating nature of Mr Dombey's pride against a background of achievement and damage wrought by that pride. With Edith the wider, public meanings do not really move with the private meanings, partly because she is so peculiar a case (unlike Mrs Skewton she is hardly a 'representative' member of a moribund aristocracy, while her significance, unlike Florence's, is not associated with the human and social values she stands for), and partly, too, because she is so inadequately realized. If she is regarded primarily as a masochist – and Dickens certainly shows she is one – the defeat of Dombey's money-pride must look like a mere accident (in a way his defeat by Carker does not). But if – as Dickens seems also to have intended – her behaviour is meant to say something about the impossibility of keeping a bargain such as she and Dombey had struck (in the way Paul's history shows children cannot be raised without regard for their emotional needs), then this theme finds neither psychological nor moral realization. Dickens was different selves at different times: a prophet concerned with the moral basis of society; a psychologist with special intuitions into the abnormal; a moralist who could enjoy pointing the irony of the Pride of Self-Laceration defeating the Pride of Self-Love; and a social observer registering the tendency of the rich middle classes to marry into the old aristocracy. Dostoevsky's selves found it more difficult to assert their independence of one another; in him the social observer had to meet the demands of the psychologist and dramatist, as was shown by his struggles to use the Umetsky story in the preliminary plans of *The Idiot*. More than that: when he looked at Russian society it was in an attempt to find the meaning and direction of Russian history. In his characters, moral and religious qualities, psychology, social position, and historical significance all had to be held in balance, and all had to be taken into account in the movement of the story. The result in *The Idiot* is an allegorical plot.

Consider Nastasia Filippovna's history. Her father, the last descendant of an old and noble family, had slaved like a convict or a muzhik to repay his heavy loans and save his mortgaged lands. Eventually the struggle proved too much for him and he died. A neighbouring land-owner of great wealth and culture took charge of Nastasia, and entrusted her to the care of his German estate-manager. The Frenchified Totsky spent most of his time abroad, but noticing on a brief visit home that his ward promised to be an uncommon beauty, he put her education in the hands of a Swiss governess. At the age of sixteen Nastasia was moved into a wooden cottage equipped with 'musical instruments, an elegant young girl's library, pictures, engravings, pencils, brushes, paints, and an astonishing lap-dog'. Totsky 'somehow' became very fond of his remote little estate, and spent three or four months there every year. Then suddenly Nastasia Filippovna's true nature was

revealed when she caught wind of a match Totsky proposed to make
and appeared at his house in St Petersburg:

> This new woman turned out, in the first place, to know and
> understand a great deal – so much so, that one could not but
> marvel where she had got such knowledge, and how she could
> have worked out such definite ideas (surely not from her young
> girl's library?). What was more, she understood the legal aspect
> of a great many things, and had a certain knowledge if not of
> the world at least of how some things are done in the world.
> In the second place, her character was not at all the same as
> before; that is to say, something timid, school-girlishly uncertain;
> sometimes fascinating with its own special playfulness and
> naïveté, at others sad and pensive, astonished, mistrustful, tearful,
> and uneasy.
>
> No: an extraordinary and unexpected creature was laughing
> here before him and stinging him with venomous sarcasms,
> openly declaring that she had never had any feeling for him in
> her heart but contempt – nauseous contempt, which began at
> once after her first surprise. (pt. I, ch. 4, pp. 48f.)

The new Nastasia was willing to risk her life to revenge herself. Rather
than face the ridicule of the world, Totsky installed her in St Petersburg, surrounded her with every luxury, yet failed to establish a hold
over her. She did not depend on the luxury, and found a strange
collection of friends: poor and funny women married to government
workers, actresses, old women, and the family of a respectable teacher.

Within Nastasia looms the Russian psyche. At one point she is
called, significantly enough, an 'extremely Russian woman' (pt. I,
ch. 11). Her father's life is the history of the Russia which had to rebuild
and regain its lands after the Tartar conquest; hers is the history of the
Russia forcefully Europeanized by Peter the Great. As it absorbed a
whole new culture, that Russia remained true to itself and to its own
beliefs, preparing to show its nature. But it was only part of the old
Russia – perhaps the best, most conscious part, but subject to tremendous strains. The whole question was whether it had the internal
resources to survive, and this question is dramatized and explored in
the choices confronting Nastasia (whose name, it is often pointed out,
means *resurrection*). Rogozhin – with his strong passions, his possessive
instinct, his old, gloomy, secretive house, and his affinity with the

Old Believers – comes from the old Russia barely affected by Peter's reforms. He can sense Nastasia Filippovna's beauty, yet hardly understands it. Gania – 'the most ordinary of men' – represents the spirit of the age: grasping, ambitious, envious, unscrupulous, and without imagination. And the Prince, who comes to free Nastasia Filippovna, is the bearer of light, or the 'new word'. He embodies the ideal, something implicit all along in Russia, which had to be given form, as a goal towards which men were striving.

The public bidding for Nastasia Filippovna is correspondingly of great significance. The publicity of the action is justified because a drama involving the whole national consciousness is being enacted. The representative modern man, Gania, has, it turns out, nothing to offer. What Rogozhin has to propose is in effect death. And Prince Myshkin offers a way to salvation. Although the basis of his offer is, as he later finds, not so much love as compassion, it is difficult to imagine any other sort of love through which Nastasia could find regeneration; to accept the Prince's offer, she must in effect accept the religious ideal. Once the significance of Nastasia Filippovna's story is recognized, the questions considered earlier, about her behaviour and about the Prince's proposal of marriage, are answered. The strange effect of electric glare in the auction scene, of which A. N. Maikov complained to Dostoevsky,[15] has its explanation. It was important to attempt to save Nastasia Filippovna, and this was a public matter. The important question was less *how* than *whether* she could be saved. The existence of Russia was threatened. The test of the ideal embodied in the Prince lies, not in his offer of marriage, but, as will be shown, in certain questions Dostoevsky raises about the nature of the ideal and about its adequacy for dealing with the situation facing Russia. The answers remain in suspense as Nastasia Filippovna hesitates between Rogozhin and Myshkin.

The ideal man: Prince Myshkin and Mr Pickwick

It was important for Russians to know their ideal: through it, Dostoevsky hoped, the disintegration of his country could be halted, and Europe led to salvation.[16] What then was the ideal Dostoevsky tried to embody? L. A. Zander has claimed that in Dostoevsky prescriptive ethics (*etika normy*), which are concerned with the actions one ought to do, are replaced by 'image ethics' (*etika obraza*),[17] meaning by this the attempt to give form in oneself to some image of perfection and, so, to achieve a certain desirable spiritual state. If the argument in the two previous sections is correct, the very structure of Dostoevsky's novel forces us to see that the ideal embodied by the Prince is not connected very closely with the way he does things. His actions, at certain crucial moments, cannot be considered so much a pattern for men to follow in their relations with one another, as an allegorization of the role the ideal might play in regenerating Russia. His proposals of marriage have less to tell us about the ideal (and in particular about compassion) than their dramatic importance would at first seem to indicate (it could be argued that the value of a spiritual state is, to a certain extent, independent of the value of the particular actions to which it leads, and Dostoevsky seems to be relying on some such distinction). Dostoevsky himself hinted that the ideal was, in some sense, an *aesthetic* one, that it had to do with states of feeling, of contemplation, of being; he hoped his hero would turn out to be a 'positively beautiful man', and, significantly, Myshkin is supposed to subscribe to the notion that 'beauty saves the world'.[18]

The main questions to be considered here are these: why did Dostoevsky see Pickwick as an embodiment of the 'perfectly beautiful'? and how did his own ideal compare with Dickens's? But they can be usefully approached by way of a more technical exercise: in what way could Pickwick and Don Quixote have helped Dostoevsky to solve the problem of the ideal man? When he was at work on Part II of the novel, approximately three months after first discussing the problem in his letter to Sonia Ivanova (cited above, p. 52), Dostoevsky referred to it again, this time in his notebooks:[19]

> How can the hero's person arouse sympathy in the reader? If Don Quixote and Pickwick can arouse sympathy and succeed, as virtuous persons, this is only because they are funny –
>
> The hero of the novel, the Prince, although not funny, has another trait that arouses sympathy   he is   !   innocent !

The problem that faced him was in essence Milton's. He had to make perfection appear plausible, yet he was prevented from drawing on major areas of human experience. His hero could not struggle to achieve the ideal (and in any event Dostoevsky had failed, with Raskolnikov and in his preliminary sketches of the 'Idiot', and indeed in subsequent

writings kept on failing, to show the redemption of a great sinner).
At the same time, the hero could not be exposed to strong tempta-
tions; if he were given too intimate a knowledge of evil his victories
might seem too easily won (we can appreciate the role of Don Quixote's
madness, Pickwick's comfortable age, and Prince Myshkin's illness,
in insulating them from life). But the interest and sympathy of the
reader had to be secured, and it had to be based on identification with
the virtue embodied by the hero, rather than on pity for him because
of the misfortunes afflicting him (as with Jean Valjean). It might be
thought that Dostoevsky's principal advance over Dickens was to
make his hero a thinking man. Certainly Myshkin's doubts, his un-
certainties, his 'double thoughts', and his thirst for knowledge help to
make him plausible, even if they have not got very much to do with
beauty. More significantly, Myshkin's imagination is caught, like
Don Quixote's, by a vision of the beautiful. But if an important part
of Don Quixote's interest has to do with the completeness and con-
nectedness of his view of the world, no tradition comparable to the
chivalric ideal was available to Dostoevsky. Even if there had been one
(and subsequently, in *The Brothers Karamazov*, he attempted to develop
a new social ideal based on the traditions of Russian monasticism),
he could not assume his readers would accept it. He dramatized this
fact in his novel (pt. IV, ch. 7): Myshkin shows least awareness of his
audience precisely when he is evoking his vision of the beauty of man
and nature (they are almost as impervious to it as the goatherds
addressed by Don Quixote). The hero had to be beautiful and interesting in himself, and not only because of the ideal he was serving.

One solution to this problem was, Dostoevsky recognized, to limit
the hero's perfection in some way, so that he would be a comic
character. As the letter to Sonia Ivanova indicates, he meant by this a
character who was 'ignorant of his own worth' (hence lacking in self-
consciousness) and who was 'laughed at' or made fun of (others too
had to be ignorant of his worth), and who, in consequence, aroused the
compassion of the reader. How could the hero's 'innocence' have the
same effect? The reasons for which Don Quixote is a great comic hero
are readily apparent. There are the windmills he mistakes for giants, and
discoveries about the whole nature of faith that he stumbles on thanks
to his vision (to Sancho's request to see Dulcinea he answers: 'If I were
to show her to you, what merit would there be in confessing so
obvious a truth?'). But all this is the result of his particular madness,

his belief in the literal truth of the world of chivalry. Dostoevsky was aware of the power which this vision held over Quixote and of his tendency to reinterpret reality rather than sacrifice any portion of it.[20] If Prince Myshkin had been equally defective in his sense of reality, there would have been a danger of debasing the ideal (Dostoevsky, unlike Cervantes, sought to defend it); and, furthermore, the ideal would not have been meaningfully tested; Myshkin had to be clear-sighted about his beliefs. He could go on believing in the fundamental goodness of Nastasia Filippovna or that the Pavlovsk trees were revelations of the divine. But he was also aware of Nastasia's tormented nature and of the difficulty of making her see 'light'. He knew, too, that the Pavlovsk trees might not have very much to offer against Ippolit's vision of a relentlessly destroying Nature.

Prince Myshkin's deficient sense of reality is, in some respects, more nearly akin to Pickwick's. Dickens's hero approaches the world with an absense of preconceptions. His whole journey is one of instruction, an attempt to 'penetrate to the hidden countries' which surround Goswell Street, and to 'find the truths which are hidden beyond'. He is an innocent, in the sense once described by Chesterton: 'Pickwick goes through life with that god-like gullibility which is the key to all adventures. The greenhorn is the ultimate victor in everything; it is he that gets most out of life. . . . The whole is unerringly expressed in one fortunate phrase – he will be always "taken in." To be taken in everywhere is to see the inside of everything. It is the hospitality of circumstance.'[21] Innocence invites disaster; from the trustfulness of Mr Pickwick and his friends results the succession of scandals, involving Mistresses Wardle, Pott, Witherfield, Dowler, and of course Bardell. At one time Mr Pickwick is even driven to suspect that he and his friends must be somehow guilty. But because innocence is vulnerable it also brings out the protective instinct in men, most conspicuously in Sam Weller's adoption of his master (ch. 22): 'You rayther want some-body to look arter you, sir, wen your judgment goes out a wisitin' '; and Mr Pickwick survives unchanged until his simple-minded belief in justice and principle takes him into the Fleet. When Dostoevsky mentioned Pickwick as a man who is 'ignorant of his own worth', he may well have had in mind this lack of worldly wisdom, this freshness, which enables Pickwick to make all sorts of discoveries about men, and to carry the happiness he unconsciously promotes into every part of society. Prince Myshkin has the same sort of openness to experience.

We find it in his relations with the nihilistic young men of St Petersburg or with the fantastic liar General Ivolgin; in his conversation with the Epanchins' doorkeeper; in the way he lets Lebedev intrigue against him; in his offer of marriage to Nastasia Filippovna. The situations he gets himself into are not, by and large, farcical; his interest in the world (and Dostoevsky's) is too serious for that. But while Dostoevsky did not want his hero to be a specifically comic one, he was right in thinking that innocence could be a similar source of interest; it was the device Dickens had used for Pickwick. By their very presence, both Myshkin and Pickwick challenge conventional notions of reality.

Innocence is, however, a dubious quality. What makes *Pickwick* still interesting for some modern readers is that it is a fable about the loss of innocence. Since Mr Pickwick is not mad he must eventually see reality. He discovers in the Fleet that not all men are well-meaning; that pain and suffering exist; that these are often undeserved. Some evils, like the office of Dodson and Fogg, will never be changed by men of good will. Myshkin does not need to discover pain and suffering; none the less his insistence on assuming that everyone (except perhaps an atheist) is somehow motivated by the wish to be good, and on offering them the chance to act in accordance with their better selves, could seem mere childishness. Innocence has to seem a real asset if we are not to aspire instead for maturity, or if we are to feel that knowledge is a loss as well as a gain. Dostoevsky safeguards his hero. Myshkin (like Pickwick) does not move in a world governed by considerations of high intelligence. Dostoevsky's portraits of rationalist man tend to be hostile (Doktorenko and, in part, Ippolit). When he does present a practical, dedicated thinking man – and both Evgeny Pavlovich Radomsky and Prince Shch. are viewed quite sympathetically – he finds it difficult to make very much of their qualities; he can see their merits, but has no real enthusiasm for them. For the most part, what Myshkin is set in opposition to is social convention (for Dostoevsky it does not embody very much traditional wisdom, nor present a very interesting surface). To all intents and purposes, the ordinary sense of reality in *The Idiot* is taken to be that of social or economic man, whereas the innocent Prince Myshkin has the wisdom of the heart (the 'principal mind'). Since he does not have to compete with mature intelligence when he acts, his innocence has considerable dramatic effectiveness.

If Dostoevsky's (and of course Dickens's) solution was simply to weight the scales in favour of innocence, we might question its interest outside the dramatic context. And here it is no longer possible to consider Prince Myshkin's innocence mainly as a technical question. It is necessary to pass to the *content* of the ideal. Myshkin's innocence, it was suggested above, comprises a knowledge of pain and suffering. It is because of the pain and suffering in Holbein's painting of the crucified Christ that he reacts so strongly to it. The suffering in Nastasia Filippovna's face makes its beauty unendurable, and gives rise to his feeling of compassion ('co-suffering' in Russian). Rogozhin is worthy of compassion because he suffers through his love for Nastasia Filippovna. The model society Myshkin formed out of village children, once upon a time high up in the Swiss mountains, was founded on compassion for the unfortunate Marie, whom the villagers despised for allowing herself to be seduced by a commercial traveller. Marie acknowledged that she was a sinner and that she deserved to suffer, performed her lowly tasks uncomplainingly, spent her days in the mountains with the cattle, and her nights in a bare cottage. Being humble, she could accept the Prince's and the children's compassion. Because of everything the children did, she died 'almost happy'; and the children celebrated her death as a sort of sacrament. In her story we have a reminder that Christ's message was for fallen man; we see, too, a possibility of imitating the Christ who took the sins of mankind on himself and died on the cross. The notion of accepting suffering and even of taking on oneself the sins of another was, Dostoevsky thought, a very Russian idea. The humble, sniffling Surikov, whom Ippolit speaks about in his 'Confession', accepts that suffering is part of man's life; his wife died for lack of medicine, and his child froze to death, yet when Ippolit blamed Surikov for being so ineffectual, he quietly, with 'humble contempt', sent Ippolit away. Once Ippolit dreamt that Surikov had inherited a fortune and did not know what to do with it; when Ippolit suggested he make a gold coffin for the dead child he agreed with tears of gratitude. He is one of the mourners, and one of the blessed. If men accepted suffering as Christ accepted his, there would be a chance society could be regenerated.[22]

The difficulty is simply that men are not humble and submissive. Ippolit questions the need for his pain and mental suffering; and to this Myshkin has no answer in which the acceptance of pain and suffering is not already presupposed (as for instance in his advice that the dying Ippolit can only 'walk past us and forgive us our happiness'). Nastasia Filippovna wants to convince herself that she deserved to suffer, and therefore behaves so as to prove she is wicked and to punish herself. She thus rejects the whole notion of suffering as something to be borne with (in the way of, say, Sonia Marmeladova). And by refusing to marry Prince Myshkin she shows she cannot accept that her fundamental nature had survived despite the suffering inflicted on her. She rebels against her own suffering and against compassion; these could be accepted only in a spirit of humility. One way in which men might offer and receive compassion is seen by the Prince in a visionary moment when to the Epanchins' gathering of friends he says: 'You know how to forget and how to forgive those who have offended you and those who have not offended you, for it is always more difficult to forgive those who have not offended one, and just because they have not offended one, so that one's complaint of them is groundless.'²³ In part, this amounts to a recognition that we incur debts to other men simply by being in a better position than they. If every man could accept he was responsible for everyone else, it would be easier for all men to accept compassion. As Myshkin explains on another occasion (pt. III, ch. 1), what Ippolit really wants is for people to forgive him and, in turn, to accept his forgiveness. But how was this state of affairs ('heaven on earth' Prince Shch. calls it) to be attained? Perhaps there was a hope if every man could laugh at himself. Compassion and humour were closely linked for Dostoevsky (as the letter about the problem of the ideal man indicates). In the same scene where Prince Myshkin calls on men to forgive those who have not offended them, he says:

'There's no reason to be embarrassed because we are funny, is there? You know, it really is true that we're funny, we're shallow, have bad habits, we're bored, don't know how to look at things, can't understand – we're all like that, all of us, you, and I, and they. And you are not offended, are you, at my telling you to your faces that you're funny? And if that's so, then aren't you good material? Do you know, to my thinking it's sometimes a good thing to be funny. In fact, it's better: it makes it easier to forgive one another, easier to be humble. One can't understand everything at once. In order to attain perfection one must begin by not understanding a great deal. And if we understand things too quickly, perhaps we shan't understand them thoroughly. I say that to you, who have already been able to understand – and not understand – so much. I am not afraid for you now. You're not angry, are you, that such a boy as me is saying such things to you?' (pt. IV, ch. 7, p. 625)

His wisdom is the kind belonging peculiarly to a child; and of course Christ's injunction to 'become as little children' comes readily to mind.

An important part of the Christian message has to do with the simple joys and the childlike virtues. In *Pickwick Papers* they were exuberantly celebrated. Since Dostoevsky admired Mr Pickwick as an embodiment of the ideal man, perhaps some, at any rate, of these joys and virtues are also part of the 'new word' brought by Prince Myshkin. One has of course to remember that *Pickwick* is a grab-bag offering with re-makes of comic scenes from eighteenth-century novels, gothic tales, a burlesque on literary circles in the provinces, a satire on elections and politics, an attack on the administration of justice and on prisons. It is only by degrees that Pickwick, with the help of Sam Weller, becomes something more than a fat man who happens to be involved in this or that adventure. And Sam's attitude to his master is important, for Sam is the spirit of life and of man; he has a great capacity for survival, and the common sense that such a capacity must imply. His appraisal of his master is neither jeering nor condescending. He sees the child inside Pickwick's old body (ch. 39): 'I never see such a fine creetur in my days. Blessed if I don't think his heart must ha' been born five-and-twenty year arter his body, at least!'

The fullest revelation of childlike joy (with elements of the childish) comes in the description of Christmas ('the season of hospitality, merriment, and open-heartedness') at Dingley Dell. Christmas is partly a regression to childhood, and to unconscious enjoyment of nature and playing. The chief misfortune that can occur is for Mr Pickwick to fall through the ice, but three bowls of punch – with its magic properties – soon restore him. Indeed, punch, good fellowship, and, of course, eating and laughter are prime ingredients of Pickwickian happiness. The Christmas tale about Gabriel Grub inserted by Dickens (in the instalment for January 1837) emphasizes that this happiness is for everyone. Grub saw (ch. 29) that 'men who worked hard, and earned their scanty bread with lives of labour, were cheerful and happy; and that to the most ignorant, the sweet face of nature was a never-failing source of cheerfulness and joy'. While the attitude to hard work and nature illustrated here may seem *childish*, an important part of the message of the whole of *Pickwick Papers*, as of the other early novels, is that the principal joys to be had are available to all men, at any rate in the boisterous moment of self-abandonment that is Christmas.

Prince Myshkin is a 'perfect child'. His doctor has told him that in 'development, soul, character, and maybe even mind' he will never be an adult (and he gets on particularly well with children). Madame Epanchina, who responds so forthcomingly to his widom of the heart, is also a child, in 'everything good and everything bad'. Gania, despite his bitterness and frustration, can still laugh like a child, and makes peace with the Prince just as a child would. Keller, a boxer who is always willing to join in a brawl, has a 'childlike trustfulness and unusual truthfulness'. There is even something childlike in the openness of Lebedev's intrigues against the Prince. In fact, almost everyone who is affected in some way, however briefly, by Prince Myshkin, has something childlike in him[24] (Rogozhin is an important exception). Ippolit is one of the nihilists; his adolescent questioning of the world, his awareness of the injustice of society, his suffering and the approach of death – all make him a rebel. But he too would like to believe all people really were kind; when Madame Epanchina is so outraged by his attacks on everyone's motives as to try and strike him (pt. II, ch. 10), he realizes this is the impulse of a childlike nature. Because of her uprightness, impulsiveness, and tenderness she is not afraid to make mistakes, to quarrel, and to make things up again. It is easy for him to make friends with her, at any rate for a while. In a world of childlike men, social divisions would hardly exist in the same way, and nihilism would lose its meaning. Ippolit's relations with Prince Myshkin and Madame Epanchina suggest that in such a world he might even be reconciled to his death, so long as he knew that men admired him for the questions he was driven to ask under the stress of illness, and knew too that they would miss him as a man of superior vision and insight. Prince Myshkin's problem is to convince Ippolit of the point of behaving as though the world really did consist of well-meaning, innocent men when in fact this world exists only as an ideal.

The relationship of Prince Myshkin and Aglaia, which unfolds in the freedom of the Pavlovsk summer life (in contrast with the St Petersburg houses and flats which seem so impenetrable), shows most fully what it is to be childlike. From the start, laughter plays an important part. When Madame Epanchina asks the Prince to relate his impressions of Switzerland, he tells about the braying donkey which woke him as his train entered Basel. Aglaia and her sisters burst out laughing, and the Prince joins in (pt. I, ch. 5). When he falls asleep on the park bench, waiting for Aglaia, he awakens to the sound of her laughter (pt. III, ch. 8). They are both such innocents that for a time neither of them recognizes, or will admit, that what they feel for each other goes by the name of love. They enjoy playing with this new sensation, as when Aglaia demands of the Prince (whom she has seen only twice before), in front of her family, whether he is asking for her hand or not. Marriage to her is something he would hardly have dreamed possible (their situation here is very different from the one in which he boldly proposed to Nastasia Filippovna) and he can only say no. Aglaia bursts out laughing so infectiously that everyone joins in, the Prince with the rest; yet from this time there is a special relationship between them which no one, themselves included, understands. At the end of the evening on which they first play at being lovers (and after the scene where the Prince jumps to Nastasia Filippovna's rescue when an officer in the Epanchins' party publicly insults her), Aglaia gives him a note telling him to meet her on the park bench next morning.

> The possibility that she loved him, 'a man like him', he would have considered monstrous. It seemed to him it was simply a prank of hers, if there was anything in it at all; but he was somehow too completely indifferent to pranks, and thought them too much in the order of things; he himself was concerned with and preoccupied with something quite different. He fully believed the words which had slipped from the General in his agitation a while ago, to the effect that she was laughing at them all, and at him, the Prince, in particular. He did not feel at all offended at this; in his opinion this was as it should be. The main thing for him was that tomorrow, early in the morning, he would see her again, would sit next to her on the green bench, hear about the loading of a pistol, and look at her. He did not need anything more. (pt. III, ch. 3, p. 410)

On a later occasion Aglaia mocks the Prince when he loses a game of chess, but grows furious when he beats her at cards, and then sends him a hedgehog as a peace-offering.

> As soon as Aglaia had got hold of the hedgehog, she packed it with Kolia's help in a woven basket, covered it with a napkin, and

started asking Kolia to carry it, at once, without stopping, to
the Prince, on her behalf, as a 'token of her deepest respect'.
Kolia joyfully agreed, and promised to deliver it, but then
started asking insistently, 'What's the meaning of the hedgehog
and why the present?' Aglaia answered that it was none of his
business. He answered he was convinced there was some hidden
allegory here. Aglaia grew angry and retorted he was just a
little boy and nothing more. Kolia immediately objected that
if he did not have some respect for her as a woman, as well as
for his own convictions, he would soon show her he knew how to
answer such an insult. In the end, however, Kolia carried the
hedgehog off triumphantly, and Kostia Lebedev ran after him.
Seeing that Kolia was waving the basket about too much, Aglaia
had to cry after him from the terrace: 'Please, dear Kolia, don't
drop it', as if she had not been quarrelling with him just before.
Kolia stopped and likewise, as if he had not been quarrelling,
called out with great readiness: 'No, I'll not drop it Aglaia
Ivanovna. Rest quite assured!' and again took off at breakneck
speed. After this Aglaia burst out laughing and ran to her room
extremely pleased, and remained very cheerful all day. (pt. IV,
ch. 5, pp. 577f.)

The Prince accepts the hedgehog in the same spirit (and it is the spirit
animating Mr Pickwick's quarrels with Mr Winkle or Mr Perker). In
laughing with one another, as well as at one another, Aglaia and
Myshkin accept one another, or – to use Dostoevsky's phrase – forgive
one another.

In the end, the idylls of Pickwick and Myshkin are destroyed – in
significantly different ways – by suffering. Inside the Fleet, Mr Pickwick
goes on a visit of the prison (ch. 45); faced with the misery, squalor, and
injustice he finds, he can only beat a retreat: ' "I have seen enough",
said Mr. Pickwick as he threw himself into a chair in his little apart-
ment. "My head aches with these scenes, and my heart too. Hence-
forth I will be a prisoner in my own room." ' When he goes to the
office of Dodson and Fogg to pay the costs of the suit they had brought
against him (ch. 53), he turns on them and attacks them as a 'well-
matched pair of mean, rascally, pettifogging robbers'. The corruption
of law, which they represent, is responsible for much of the misery
he has witnessed. After this his countenance is again 'smiling and

placid', and he is able to laugh with his friends. With reference to the Dickens of *Pickwick Papers*, Edmund Wilson has claimed that his 'laughter is an exhilaration which already shows a trace of the hysterical'.[25] Whether or not this is so, it is difficult to accept that the laughter in this scene is of the same cheerful kind as before; it has become a release for frustration. At the same time, Pickwick's charity – in his treatment of Mr Jingle and Mrs Bardell – shows a new maturity. He can never be quite the same again; he loses his childlike innocence, or loses his right to it. Myshkin, of course, knows about suffering from the start. But he is engaged in a desperate attempt to preserve his childlike delight in the world alongside this knowledge. In his world there must be room for Aglaia *and* Nastasia Filippovna. But what is the place of suffering and compassion in the childlike vision? It is true that the village children, led by Myshkin, did create a whole life for themselves based on compassion. Surely, though, compassion could not have the same meaning for them as for the Prince; everything they did for him was (as he admits) part of a marvellous fairy-tale in which the Prince was secretly in love with Marie (and he did not wish to undeceive them).[26] There is too much of the adult in Aglaia for her to lead a fairy-tale life. She is willing to take the Prince, with all his awkwardness and absurdity, and so to accept the childlike ideal, but she realizes there is something terribly serious about the Prince's compassion, and is afraid it will always have the stronger hold on his nature (significantly, when he is asleep on the park bench he is being tormented by a vision of Nastasia's unhappiness at the very moment Aglaia stands before him laughing).[27] She has good reason to fight so furiously against Nastasia in the highly melodramatic confrontation of the two women (pt. IV, ch. 8). Because Nastasia's suffering is a threat, Aglaia tries to discredit the whole basis of her rival's behaviour. She is right about Nastasia's wish to make a martyr of herself, although in levelling this charge she lacks charity and humility; the child in her is destroyed. And she is right about Myshkin; when he is faced with the crucial choice, he pauses to look at Nastasia's suffering countenance, and in effect makes his decision.

The choice confronting Myshkin dramatizes one of the basic difficulties in Christianity, or at any rate in Dostoevsky's Christianity. If we are as children, can we really understand Christ's agony and death on the cross? And if we are filled with the meaning of the crucifixion, can we ever go back to being children? This contradiction is embodied

in an image sketched by Nastasia Filippovna in one of her letters to
Aglaia:

> I would leave him with just one small child. The child has been
> playing next to Him; maybe he has been telling Him something
> in his child-language. Christ has been listening to him, but has
> now grown thoughtful. His hand has remained unconsciously,
> forgetfully, on the child's fair [*svetlyi*] head. He is looking into
> the distance, at the horizon; a thought, great as the whole world,
> rests in His glance; His face is sad. The child has become silent
> and is leaning against His knees; with his cheek propped on his
> hand, he raises his head, and pensive – the way children sometimes
> are – he gazes at Him. (pt. III, ch. 10, pp. 516f.)

Prince Myshkin attempts to combine both sorts of awareness. But
Aglaia knows that Nastasia Filippovna will always be a threat to
Eden and that, because of her, the Prince's impulses will never be free
from internal conflict. And Nastasia Filippovna comes to realize that
she is forever cut off from Eden; her mere presence is enough to destroy
it. Prince Myshkin's attempt is the source of his appeal for the other
characters. The impossibility of his task is, perhaps, the source of his
appeal for us; we seem to have an instinct requiring that perfection be
doomed before we value it.

There is a basic conflict between suffering and the childlike world. If
they are to co-exist, either the intensity of suffering, or the intensity of
joy, or both, must be reduced. In *Pickwick Papers* the intensity of suffering is, in comparison with *The Idiot*, never very strong; Mr Pickwick's
delight in the world can in certain measure survive his exposure to the
Fleet. Prince Myshkin, who is aware of suffering from the start, has in
the end to face the basic contradiction in his aspirations; his escape lies
in madness. Dickens leaves Pickwick and his companions with the
light 'blazing full upon them'. We remember that the sun has accom-
panied Mr Pickwick in his travels, and that he is himself a dispenser of
light and warmth. Prince Myshkin's light (which is referred to over and
over again in all sorts of contexts) is eclipsed by darkness. It may seem
appropriate that in England the childlike ideal should better survive
than in the Russia of Alexander II (and also that there is less of the
spiritual in it). Or perhaps *Pickwick* was the kind of novel only an
author who was himself still an innocent could write; in his later
novels, Dickens came to write of a society where work was not

always available, where even when it was it was not productive of real happiness, and where benevolence was no longer sufficient to heal the divisions of society. In these novels the Pickwickian ideal all but disappeared. As for Dostoevsky's attitude towards *Pickwick*, while it cannot be set forth in detail, we can hardly doubt that it had to do with the childlike vision.

Allegorical patterns and myth

Allegory was close to the imagination of nineteenth-century writers and readers in Russia. In part this was a response to censorship. If social and political questions could not be openly handled they could be dealt with under the mantle of literature and criticism. Belinsky and his school were always discussing what literature had to show about the condition of Russia and the needs of the country. For example, Dobroliubov[28] saw the heroine of Turgenev's *On the Eve* as an image of that element in Russian society which had become aware of the prevailing misery, injustice, and arbitrary power, and which was looking for some effective way of doing good; her feelings of dissatisfaction and confinement in the society round her led her to embrace the ideals of a Bulgarian nationalist fighting for the freedom of his country. Dobroliubov stressed the allegorical element in this story, and invited an allegorical reading of his own criticism by saying provocatively, or reassuringly, that Elena could not have found her hero in a Russian. But allegory was more than a device adopted by radical and progressive critics in the discussion of literature (often without regard to the appropriateness of the device). It is perhaps a natural growth where a collision of cultures exists. An ordinary realistic framework can hardly do justice to the life of the imagination under such conditions; the questions men feel to be important are too far-reaching. Chaadaev's famous 'Philosophical Letter' had made Russians wonder where they stood in relation to Europe: the clerk who went mad in Pushkin's 'The Bronze Horseman' was a victim of the alien civilization imposed on Russia by an iron-willed Tsar; the troika in which Chichikov made his exit from *Dead Souls* was refined by Gogol into a symbol of Russia and her strange destiny.

There is an allegorizing tendency in much of Dostoevsky's work. The Karamazov family is an image of all Russia. *The Gambler* demands to be interpreted in terms of a Russia squandering its resources and unable to find itself; the symbolical significance of the grandmother, of the young Russians Polina and Aleksei, of the Frenchman de Grieux, and of the Englishman Astley is at once apparent. It seems that in composing his novels Dostoevsky often had to find general significance before proceeding to particular behaviour and characteristics; a decisive phase was reached in *The Idiot* when Dostoevsky jotted down the two words 'Prince Holy-Fool' in his notebooks.[29] Further evidence that his method of thought is in part allegorical (although not in the sense – in which he himself uses the word – of a moral or thesis which was not artistically realized) is contained in this statement:[30]

> Of course, allegory is unthinkable in such an artistic work, as, for example, *Notre Dame de Paris*. But to whom will it not occur that Quasimodo is a personification of the oppressed and despised French people of the Middle Ages, dumb and disfigured, endowed only with fearful physical strength, but in whom, at last, there awakens love, and a thirst for justice, and at the same time a consciousness of their truth and of their untried, boundless strength.

Dostoevsky had an allegorical imagination. But is the interpretation of *The Idiot* offered here a correct one? There have been others. Zander thinks that Myshkin makes his proposal to Nastasia because he embodies in himself an image of Christ – the Heavenly Bridegroom. 'His tragedy is that life and maybe his own self have placed him in the situation of "bridegroom" when there is only one "Bridegroom"; there can be none other, and anybody who willingly or unwillingly assumes this role must inevitably perish.'[31] There are certain difficulties in this view. It implies that in depicting the ideal Dostoevsky had a definite image to imitate, whereas part of his problem was to find and give form to (*izobrazit'*) the ideal Russians had kept in their hearts. It does not seem to allow in any convenient way for Myshkin's relations with Aglaia; it takes an aspect of Christ related to his heavenly rather than his human role; and it suggests that Myshkin really is one of Dostoevsky's great heresiarchs (one or two critics have based their interpretation on this hint of Zander's, but surely such a view is too obviously eccentric to need refutation). What one might say along the lines of Zander's interpretation is that the reconciliation of incompatibles – of suffering and of childlike joy – attempted by Jesus is impossible in a human world. If the Christian myth has any power it must be in relation to Jesus Christ, the God-man. The problem of the

God-man and of man-gods becomes important in Dostoevsky's subsequent works.

The allegorical significance of *The Idiot* extends to the other main characters. Through her mother Aglaia descends from an ancient Russian family related to Prince Myshkin's. Her father, the General, is a self-made man, who has risen through the ranks, and has acquired various industrial interests. While her parents move in aristocratic circles, they are not bound by conventions, and are not afraid to find friends elsewhere. Aglaia says that their social position is 'as middle as can be'.[32] She herself has access to people in every part of society; her friends include the young Kolia Ivolgin and the nihilistic Ippolit. She quotes Pushkin readily and with feeling; and Radomsky speaks for Dostoevsky in saying that Pushkin and one or two others were the only Russian writers to have said something distinctively their own (but Dostoevsky knew how much European forms and influences counted for in this achievement). Aglaia inherits by right what is best in the Russian tradition. Significantly, she shares two of Nastasia Filippovna's suitors (Myshkin and Gania). And the possibility of her marriage to Myshkin is twice raised in almost as public a context as his proposal to Nastasia. 'Allow me, mam-ma to speak; I count for something in this matter: an extraordinary moment of my fate is being decided – these were the words Aglaia used – and I want to find out for myself, and I am glad, besides, that it's in front of everyone.'[33] In the pattern of the story, Aglaia stands for the new – as Nastasia for the old – psyche of Russia.

The epileptic Prince is the bearer of enlightenment. Although he has to discover his homeland, he is a very Russian figure, and can readily recognize the characteristic manifestations of religious feeling in Russia. At the same time he is not provincial in his significance. Holbein's painting of Christ in the Tomb represents one of the severest tests of his faith; a Swiss doctor has saved him from incoherence; and his ideal was first discovered abroad. He is willing to step aside and let Rogozhin marry Nastasia, in the hope that they both can be brought to the light. But Rogozhin (though he has read Pushkin together with Myshkin, and reads Soloviev's *History of Russia* at the behest of Nastasia) remains a figure of darkness; when he appears before Ippolit (pt. III, ch. 6), who can neither reconcile himself to a destructive universe nor find anything else to believe in, he comes as the devil (it is odd that Ippolit describes him as a man leading the 'fullest, most spontaneous life' when Rogozhin is so completely a prisoner of his possessive instincts). Nastasia, in turn, is willing to marry Rogozhin so that Aglaia and Myshkin can find happiness together. In effect, she is willing to sacrifice herself for the sake of innocence and the new psyche. But in the end she is no more capable of self-sacrifice than of regeneration; she agrees to marry Myshkin, then at the last moment escapes with Rogozhin, and meets her death. The old psyche cannot survive; and at the same time the new psyche is destroyed by the burden of the past. Aglaia, who might have been a personification of a regenerated Russia, marries a Polish Catholic supposedly condemned to live abroad because of his anti-Russian activities, who in the end turns out to be no aristocrat or revolutionary, but an out-and-out scoundrel. In terms of the whole novel, it seems right that neither the old nor the new Russia should have a chance. The country was being invaded with ideas from the West, and as the nihilistic young men of St Petersburg demonstrate, it was less and less able to absorb them.

The shifts in the story are worked out through the psychology of the characters. The underlying allegory is probably something towards which Dostoevsky felt his way in the course of writing and publishing, rather than something he deliberately introduced. This explains why, in his notebooks, he considered so many different developments of the plot.[34] At one stage, he thought the Prince would actually marry Nastasia; at another – Aglaia. He also entertained the idea of Aglaia marrying Gania; of Rogozhin falling in love with Aglaia; of Gania strangling Aglaia; and of Aglaia helping the Prince to rehabilitate Nastasia. He was not very clear about what to do with Gania, and contemplated making him into a character of 'colossal seriousness', a 'terrible character'. But then he seems to have realized that Gania's main significance had to do with the struggle for Nastasia's hand and then for Aglaia's, and that to make him into a tragic character would needlessly complicate the pattern. The emergence of Ippolit (who at times is closely identified with Gania) is probably to be attributed to this; he supplies a need which could not be filled by any of the characters in the main plot, and he raises many of the questions to which the Prince's 'new word' must give an answer.

The movement of the central plot in *The Idiot* shows there was little hope for the regeneration of Russia. Salvation could only be an individual matter. Specially significant in this connection are the anecdotes Prince Myshkin tells about the Russians he has met on his journeys (pt. II, ch. 4): the peasant who prayed to God as he cut his friend's throat; the soldier who sold the Prince a tin cross, pretending that it was silver (but for whom the symbol of the cross possibly still had some meaning); and the peasant woman who compared her own joy at seeing her baby smile with the joy God felt when a sinner turned to him. But for Russia as a whole the signs were ominous. While the society depicted by Dostoevsky is still, on the surface, a stable one, its failure to understand what the Prince is trying to do is portentous. The Prince moves in an atmosphere of gossip and scandal. After the scenes at Nastasia Filippovna's with the burning of the hundred thousand roubles, and later after the scene at the Epanchins' with the breaking of the Chinese vase, all sorts of strange stories circulate. For instance, according to rumours about the auction scene: 'Some princeling or simpleton (nobody knew his name) had suddenly received an enormous inheritance and married a visiting Frenchwoman, a famous can-can dancer from the Château-de-Fleurs in Paris. Others said that some general had received the inheritance, and that it was a Russian merchant of untold wealth who had married the famous can-can dancer, and that, out of mere swaggering, he had burned lottery tickets worth a round sum of seven hundred thousand roubles over a candle.' The breaking of the vase and Myshkin's treatment of Aglaia are seen as acts of deliberate nihilism.[35] With few exceptions (Madame Epanchina is one and at the end Radomsky is possibly another) the Russians in the novel understood neither the compassionate ideal nor the childlike one. It is as though Dostoevsky were looking for a life-enhancing or life-saving myth, turning on the mysteries of death, sacrifice, and rebirth. But his fable could only be demoniac; and correspondingly, the imagination of nineteenth-century Russians was demoniac or, worse, blind.

Notes

1   *Iz arkhiva F. M. Dostoevskogo: Idiot, Neizdannye materialy*, ed. P. N. Sakulin and N. F. Bel'chikov (Moscow-Leningrad, 1931).
2   *Dombey*, ch. 21, p. 293; ch. 43, p. 611. Not surprisingly the second, long passage gave Vvedensky some trouble in his translation, but both here and elsewhere he got the important meanings.
3   *The Idiot*, pt. III, ch. 8, pp. 492f. (in *Sobranie sochinenii*, vol. 6).
4   Pt. IV, ch. 8, p. 641; ch. 9, p. 657.
5   *Dombey*, ch. 45, p. 626; ch. 47, p. 657; *The Idiot*, pt. I, ch. 4, p. 49.

6   *Dombey*, ch. 35, p. 501; *The Idiot*, pt. I, ch. 4, p. 57; ch. 13, p. 156. In translating 'bargain' and 'recompense' Vvedensky uses the same words as Dostoevsky's *plata* and *voznagrazhdenie*.
7   *Dombey*, ch. 54, p. 763; *The Idiot*, pt. IV, ch. 9, p. 656.
8   *Dombey*, ch. 30, p. 432; ch. 54, p. 764. *The Idiot*, pt. I, ch. 16, p. 199.
9   *Dombey*, ch. 43, p. 611; *The Idiot*, pt. I, ch. 16, pp. 194, 198. Other parallels: Edith's wedding is like a funeral and Nastasia's becomes a funeral; each woman has for suitor an ambitious man of the new age who seeks to humiliate her by way of compensation for past restraint (Gania, Carker).
10 'Dombey and Son', *Sewanee Review*, 70 (1962).
11 'Dickens in Relation to Criticism', *Fortnightly Review*, 17 (1872).
12 *Charles Dickens* (London, 1906), p. 168.
13 Ch. 40, p. 565; ch. 42, p. 603.
14 See A. S. Dolinin, 'Dostoevsky i Suslova', in his collection *F. M. Dostoevsky: Stat'i i materialy*, vol. 2 (Leningrad, 1924).
15 See *Pis'ma*, vol. 2, p. 419.
16 See for instance *Diary of a Writer* (1877), January, ch. 2, i, and also the Pushkin Speech.
17 *Taina dobra* (Frankfurt, 1960), pp. 23f., 116ff.
18 Pt. III, ch. 5, p. 433.
19 *Idiot, Neizdannye materialy*, ed. Sakulin and Bel'chikov, p. 120.
20 See 'Lying Saves a Lie', *Diary of a Writer* (1877), September.
21 *Charles Dickens*, p. 98.
22 *The Idiot*, pt. I, ch. 6, pp. 79–85; ch. 7, pp. 92f.; pt. II, ch. 4, pp. 247f.; ch. 5, pp. 261f.; pt. III, ch. 6, pp. 449f., 462.
23 Quoted from the original edition of the novel in *Russkii vestnik* (December 1869, p. 756). The longer passage quoted below came immediately before.
24 *The Idiot*, pt. I, ch. 6, pp. 86, 88f.; ch. 11, p. 143; pt. II, ch. 11, p. 351.
25 *The Wound and the Bow* (Cambridge, Mass., 1941), p. 14.
26 Pt. I, ch. 6, p. 83.
27 The compassion sometimes turns into an obsession with suffering. There is a strong undercurrent of rejection of the world which carries the novel away at several points (as when Myshkin acts in such a way as to invite Rogozhin to murder him).
28 In a review in *Sovremennik* (1860).
29 *Idiot, Neizdannye materialy*, p. 76.
30 *Stat'i*, p. 526.
31 *Taina dobra*, p. 129.
32 Pt. IV, ch. 6, p. 593.
33 Pt. IV, ch. 5, p. 581.
34 *Idiot, Neizdannye materialy*, pp. 96, 100, 108f., 146, 152.
35 Pt. II, ch. 1, pp. 204f.; pt. IV, ch. 9, pp. 648ff.

5

The Idiot:
reality

It seemed to me that if you were to go straight on, for a long, long
time, and go beyond that line, the actual line, where heaven meets earth,
the whole solution would lie there, and straight away you would see a
new life, a thousand times stronger and noisier than ours. I was always
dreaming of a big town, like Naples, where there were palaces, noise,
thunder, and life – But what didn't I dream of? And then it came to me
that even in prison you could find tremendous life.[1]

Little Dorrit *and the condition of Russia*

The Nastasia-Myshkin-Aglaia story in *The Idiot* is used by Dostoevsky
to explore the Russian ideal and the Russian past and present, and thus
to impose a structure on his novel. As he works out the central fable,
he exposes Prince Myshkin to the real world, and tests the power of the
ideal to transform it. But rich as the book is in allegoric and realistic
modes, not much in it prepares us for the journalistic piece about the
state of Russia which opens Part III:

There are continual complaints that we have no practical men;
that there are, for instance, many politicians, also many generals,
and officials of various kinds can be found at once, in any number,
however many are required. But, as for practical men, there are
none. At any rate, everybody complains there are none. They say
there is not even a decent railway servant on some lines; that it's
quite impossible to set up the least bit tolerable management in
any kind of steamer-company. . . . There seem to be so many
posts in the government service, that it is frightening to think of
it. Everybody has been in the service, is in the service, is going
to be in the service – so how, with all this material, can some
kind of decent steamer-company management not be formed?

To this an extremely simple answer is sometimes given – so simple an answer that it can hardly be believed. Namely: it's true that everyone has been or is in the service, and that this has been going on for the past two hundred years, according to the best German pattern, from great-grandfather to great-grandson – but the men in the service are the most unpractical of people, so much so, that abstract views and a lack of practical knowledge were quite recently regarded, even in the service, as great virtues and recommendations. However, it is no use speaking of men in the service, since, actually, we wanted to speak of practical men. Here there can be no doubt that diffidence and complete lack of initiative have constantly been regarded by us as the foremost and best sign of a practical man – and are even now so regarded. But why accuse just ourselves? – if, indeed, this opinion is an accusation. Everywhere, all over the world, from the dawn of time, lack of originality has been regarded as the prime attribute and best recommendation of a sensible, business-like, practical man, and at least ninety-nine per cent of mankind (at the very least) have always held to this view, while possibly one per cent always have taken and do take a different one.

Social journalism of this kind is a favourite device of Dickens's for extending or bringing out the meaning of his stories. Could he be the influence behind Dostoevsky's bold introduction of seemingly extraneous material? Certainly the social attitudes which Dostoevsky exposes (and clearly enjoys exposing) are close to those denounced in the onslaught on the Circumlocution Office in *Little Dorrit*:[2]

This glorious establishment had been early in the field, when the one sublime principle involving the difficult art of governing a country, was first distinctly revealed to statesmen. It had been foremost to study that bright revelation, and to carry its shining influence through the whole of the official proceedings. Whatever was required to be done, the Circumlocution Office was beforehand with all the public departments in the art of perceiving – HOW NOT TO DO IT.

Through this delicate perception, through the tact with which it invariably seized it, and through the genius with which it always acted on it, the Circumlocution Office had risen to

over-top all the public departments; and the public condition had
risen to be – what it was. . . .

. . . It was this spirit of national efficiency in the
Circumlocution Office that had gradually led to its having
something to do with everything. Mechanicians, natural
philosophers, soldiers, sailors, petitioners, memorialists, people
with grievances, people who wanted to redress grievances, jobbing
people, jobbed people, people who couldn't get rewarded for
merit, and people who couldn't get punished for demerit, were
all indiscriminately tucked up under the foolscap paper of the
Circumlocution Office.

There are of course differences. Dickens is himself a master of the art of
'How not to do it', and in telling us how not to do things, he lets us
know a certain amount about how they are done, and how he thinks
they should be done. Dostoevsky (as will be brought out below) is
much closer to the Russian 'liberals' discussed by Radomsky and
Myshkin who attack 'not the existing order of things, but the very
essence of things' (pt. III, ch. 1). Then too Dostoevsky does not
personify general attitudes in the manner of Dickens with the Barnacles,
who administer the Circumlocution Office. Had he done so, it might
have been too direct an attack on the government; in any event his
characters were too complex in their motives and desires to lend
themselves to this simple sort of personification.

The similarities need no underlining. And Dostoevsky's complaint
that 'inventors and geniuses have always been regarded as fools'[3]
might be an allusion to the sufferings of Daniel Doyce at the hands of
the Barnacle Tribe. Moreover, the whole social outlook of the two
authors comes closer in these books than anywhere else. Both novels
have at the centre of the action a childlike figure who has to contend
with the world of nineteenth-century capitalism. (*Little Dorrit* stands
out among Dickens's novels in this respect; the world Pickwick moves
in is, for instance, not essentially different from that of the tourist.)
There is a fever for speculation and investments. Millionaires (Merdle,
Rogozhin) are literally worshipped; everything can be bought.
Rigaud proclaims: 'I sell everything that commands a price. . . .
Society sells itself and sells me: and I sell society'; likewise Rogozhin:
'I have money, brother, lots of money. . . . If I want to, I will buy
everyone! I will buy everything!'[4] Political economy is the ruling
ideology, and the poor are no longer to be considered:

> Some of 'em will pull long faces to me, and say, Poor as you see
> us, master, we're always grinding, drudging, toiling, every
> minute we're awake. I say to them, What else are you made for?
> It shuts them up. They haven't a word to answer. What else are
> we made for? That clinches it. (Pancks, in *Little Dorrit*, bk. I,
> ch. 13, p. 160)
> All of them point to their working-men's hands, get angry, and
> shout, 'We labour like oxen, and toil, and we're hungry as dogs
> and poor. The others don't labour and toil, but they're rich!'
> (the eternal refrain)! . . . Oh, I've never, then or now, felt any
> pity for these idiots – I say it with pride! (Ippolit, in *The Idiot*,
> pt. III, ch. 5, pp. 445f.)

Under the weight of this ideology (and of the Circumlocution Office
men) there is a danger of society collapsing. As Pancks says: 'Keep me
always at it, and I'll keep you always at it, you keep somebody else
always at it. There you are with the Whole Duty of Man in a commercial country.' Lebedev challenges the defenders of the theory to
explain how they are going to 'save the world' with their 'science,
industry, associations, and wage-packets'; he asserts that everything is
falling apart, and that the laws of self-preservation and of self-destruc-
tion are really the same.[5] The shadow of the Apocalypse lies over
England as over Russia. It is a time of false prophets and gods; Casby
is a Patriarch, and Merdle an Apostle, while Gania is King of the Jews;
the passion for investments is an epidemic or plague; the network of
railways spreading over Russia is identified with the star called Worm-
wood. In both novels darkness seems to cover the land.

Both authors set out to combat this state of affairs – to find some
place for the ideal in the world as it is. An ideal society can exist readily
enough in isolation – in the Marshalsea prison; or in the monastery on
the Great St Bernard, to which the Dorrits travel; or in the Swiss
mountain village where Myshkin goes for treatment. The problem is
to recreate such a community in the outside world. And in both novels
there is a strong sense that people must stay at home and work. Abroad,
the Dorrits have cut themselves off from any meaningful life. Perhaps
this is nowhere better expressed than in Little Dorrit's experience of the
strangeness of Venice:

> In this crowning unreality, where all the streets were paved with
> water, and where the deathlike stillness of the days and nights was

broken by no sound but the softened ringing of the church-bells,
the rippling of the current, and the cry of the gondoliers turning
the corners of the flowing streets, Little Dorrit, quite lost by her
task being done, sat down to muse. . . . She would watch the
sunset, in its long low lines of purple and red, and its burning
flush high up into the sky: so glowing on the buildings, and so
lightening their structure, that it made them look as if their strong
walls were transparent, and they shone from within. . . . And then
she would lean upon her balcony, and look over at the water . . .
as if, in the general vision, it might run dry, and show her the
prison again, and herself, and the old room, and the old inmates,
and the old visitors: all lasting realities that had never changed.
(bk. II, ch. 3, p. 467)

Madame Epanchina's words that close *The Idiot* strike the same note:
'We've spent time enough distracting ourselves; now it's time to hear
reason. And all this, all this "abroad" and all of your Europe, it is all
just fantasy, and all of us abroad are just fantasy. Mark my words.
You'll see yourself.'

But was *Little Dorrit* an influence that permeates the whole of *The
Idiot* and is manifested in the countless points of similarity? There is
no way of telling. To speak of such an influence we should need to
know a fair amount about Dostoevsky's opinions on *Little Dorrit*,
and in none of his extant references to Dickens is this novel even
specifically mentioned, although an urgent recommendation to read it
was given him by his brother Michael in 1859 (when Dostoevsky was
living in exile in Tver).[6] None the less, internal evidence in *The Idiot*
is good enough to show that Dickens's novel entered into its composition in certain tangential ways. And while we can never know
whether, say, he was thinking of the imprisoning state of mind of the
masochistic and rebellious Miss Wade when he endowed Nastasia with
her sense of being in a prison, the suggestion that his social journalism
derives from Dickens's can be made into a compelling one.

Practical men and benevolence

In the light of what Dostoevsky has to say about the treatment of
inventors and geniuses in the opening to Part III of *The Idiot*, we might
expect him to make a great deal of Prince Shch., who is 'desirous of the

useful' and who is 'distinguished by that rare and happy virtue of
always finding work'. But after a warm introduction (in pt. II, ch. 11),
Dostoevsky does scarcely anything with him, yet surely he was sincere
in praising the Prince, and was complaining in his own voice about the
shortage of practical men. His letter to A. N. Maikov of 20 March/2
April 1868 shows that the subject was exercising his mind:[7]

> I have been reading *Golos*. Terribly sad facts are related there
> at times. For instance, the mess with our railways (just built),
> *zemstvo* affairs, the sorry state of the colonies. It is a terrible
> misfortune we still have so few people who can carry things
> out. There are talkers, but to do things – hardly anyone. Of
> course, I don't mean people to carry out the big business, but
> simply small employees, who are needed in large numbers but
> are lacking. Perhaps there are enough people for the courts and
> juries. But what about the railways? And elsewhere. There is
> a terrible collision between the old order and the new people and
> new requirements. I've no need to speak about the ideas animating
> them: there are a lot of free-thinkers, but no Russian people.
> Above all: the consciousness of being a Russian man – that is
> what is needed. Publicity – Lord! even of the Westernizing,
> hostile kind – will help the Tsar and all Russians. I so much
> want the railways along political lines to be built quickly
> . . . and also guns.

It seems there was a disjunction between the man and the artist (was it a
sense of spite, resulting from failure, that led Dostoevsky to attribute
shallow aristocratic airs to Prince Shch.?). But Dostoevsky did have an
idea of what the 'practical' qualities were, as will appear from the odd
statement in which his journalistic exercise in *The Idiot* culminates:

> In fact only an original or in other words restless man can fail
> to become a general in our country. . . . None the less, we have
> said much too much; actually we wanted to say a few words
> about our acquaintances, the Epanchin family. These people, or at
> any rate the more rational members of the family, continually
> suffered from a family characteristic which they held more or less
> in common, and which was the opposite of the virtues we have
> just been discussing. Without completely understanding why (it
> was difficult to understand) they sometimes suspected things did

not run in their family the way they did for everyone else. For
everyone things went smoothly – for them, bumpily. Everybody
was sliding along rails – while they were continually jumping
the rails. Everyone constantly displayed a well-mannered diffidence
– but they – no, not they. It is true that Lizaveta Prokofevna was
even excessively afraid, but this was not that well-mannered
diffidence for which they longed. (pt. III, ch. 1, p. 369)

The attack on the bureaucratic attitudes responsible for the social and
economic decay of Russia seems to be set up in order to reveal the
qualities of true originality, such as characterize the Epanchins. It is as
though the Epanchins have the necessary practical qualities. What
Dostoevsky specially values in them must have something to do with
their refusal to be bound by prejudices of caste, and with their willingness to act on what they feel is right. Because of this, Prince Myshkin
is able to reveal himself to them more fully than to anybody else, so
soon after meeting them. And also because of this, Madame Epanchina
(Lizaveta Prokofevna) intervenes so that Aglaia shall treat the Prince
in accordance with his merits and with what she, Aglaia, really feels
for him, even though as a mother Madame Epanchina is tortured by
the idea of marrying her daughter to so outlandish a person. The
sudden switch to the Epanchins might seem to suggest that Dostoevsky
has raised the questions about the social, political, and economic
situation of Russia only to dismiss them. This is true to the extent that
for Dostoevsky the social and economic questions are secondary; they
follow on the spiritual ones. For the purposes of the novel, the Epanchins are the practical people, because they can recognize true originality, and because they have the spiritual qualities that really matter:
childlike honesty, spontaneity, and a measure of innocence.

The Epanchins serve a purpose strangely like that of the 'practical' Pa
and Ma Meagles in *Little Dorrit*. After his frustrating visit to the
Circumlocution Office, Clennam runs into Mr Meagles and the
inventor Daniel Doyce, who is treated as a public offender for 'trying
to turn his ingenuity to his country's service'. Meagles, a practical man,
defends Doyce against the Barnacles (although Meagles – a retired
banker – is himself inclined to regard the inventor as somewhat un-
sound). But the real reason why Meagles and his wife are 'practical'
is because of all the kind and spontaneous things they do (and also,
because of their tendency to take refuge in whimsy when no action is

possible). In speaking of his wife's suggestion that they adopt a child from the Foundling Hospital, Mr Meagles says: 'Now that was practical in Mother, and I told her so.' By means of this rather coy trick, Dickens is obviously suggesting that the charitable virtues should equally be regarded as practical ones in society. But he no longer places too much reliance on the Good Rich Men. Work and initiative assume a new importance in this novel, and in the union of Meagles, Clennam, Doyce, and Little Dorrit, a new basis for the community of the humble is found.[8]

In attacking bureaucratic attitudes Dostoevsky and Dickens want to assert the importance of similar 'practical' virtues (and they make use of a similar play on words to do so). Hence, the possibility that Dostoevsky's satire on the attitudes of his society was inspired by Dickens looks a likely one. The net effect is, of course, rather different. Dickens tries to build on, or rather within, the existing social order, excluding everything the Circumlocution Office and the Merdles stand for. It might seem Dostoevsky was attempting to do the same, inasmuch as the Epanchins are meant to represent some sort of 'middle rank' in Russian society[9] and the General owns a factory and has considerable practical experience of life. But if we consider Dostoevsky's attitude towards any kind of capitalist, and his express feelings about generals, it will be seen that the qualities for which Dostoevsky admires the Epanchins have more to do with his wife and daughters than with the General. And because of his inability to make anything of the other practical men in the novel, originality and inventiveness look more subversive than he probably intended.

The Epanchins and the Meagles are related in certain other ways. Both families attach a little too much importance to social values, and in consequence are humiliated. For deriving a measure of satisfaction from his daughter's marriage to an impecunious member of the Barnacle family, Mr Meagles exposes himself to being patronized and snubbed. The Epanchins feel compelled to introduce Myshkin to society (represented by some aristocrats and high government officials), and the evening ends in disaster. The families also play a similar structural role. Because they are rooted in their societies and stand for what is most worthwhile in them, they can help Clennam and Myshkin – who both after many years abroad return home in search of some field of action – to find a position in society. In each family there is a daughter (Pet, Aglaia) who awakens in the hero a forgotten or unsuspected capacity for love. And in each case the hero is introduced through them to a rival (Henry Gowan, Gania Ivolgin) who is an ambitious and frustrated man coming from a family of declining fortunes (as it turns out Myshkin and Gania are rivals for Nastasia's hand, as well as for Aglaia's). Myshkin goes to Gania's home, where he hears Madame Ivolgina discuss her son's marriage, of which she disapproves. Clennam visits Gowan's mother, and submits to having her discuss Gowan's marriage, of which she affects to disapprove. The points of similarity do suggest the possibility that some of the patterns in Dostoevsky's novel derive from *Little Dorrit,* and that his attack on attitudes and institutions is an echo – a somewhat hollow one – of Dickens's.

Individuals: Dorrit and Ivolgin

In one of the big, public discussions of the state of Russia which arise in the course of *The Idiot,*[10] it is hinted that political economy is little short of institutionalized cannibalism, and the whole scientific and practical tendency of the past centuries – a curse. There is no 'connecting idea' to hold society together. This message is borne out, in all sorts of ways, throughout the novel, and to start with – in the central fable. We must accordingly look with particular interest at Prince Myshkin's encounters and attempts to deal with individual men. Of the characters he meets in situations not directly connected with the main plot, three are specially prominent: Ippolit, Lebedev, and General Ivolgin. Ippolit's nihilism lays society open to 'the rule of the first'. Like Ivan Karamazov he is a great justifier of rebellion. His arguments are unanswerable; there is no way of proving the universe is beneficent, one can only experience it as such (Dickens embodied the same forces of discontent in Miss Wade and Tattycoram). Lebedev is a divided man, decent in his family life, ignoble in his other relations. He embodies the wealth of imagination and the chaos of Russia; he can account for modern society in terms of political economy or of the Apocalypse, but lacks any firm basis for self-judgment. He is like the rent-collector Pancks; both men understand the doctrine of self-interest and live by its rules, yet are aware of the injustice it produces. They are distinctively men of the modern world in one further respect: they live in a fragmented society, in which rumour, newspapers, and publicity supply some of the chief links between men; thanks to information picked up from these sources, Lebedev and Pancks play an important part in their respective plots.

General Ivolgin is the character confronting us with the most interesting moral questions. Mario Praz[11] has stated that he 'recalls Micawber with one or two of the characteristics of William Dorrit'. Certainly the first meeting between Prince Myshkin and the General has a very Micawberish feel. There is a description of the General coming into the Prince's room, wearing shabby clothes, smelling of vodka, and with an 'effective, rather rehearsed manner, and with an obvious fervent wish to produce an impression of dignity'. He goes up to the Prince, scrutinizes his features as if to trace a familiar face in them, takes him by the hand, and exclaims softly but solemnly: 'Himself! Himself! As if alive! I heard a well-known and beloved name repeated, and remembered the irrecoverable past. Prince Myshkin is it not?' The General could equally well have been cast in the part of Mr Micawber exclaiming 'Good Heaven, Mr Traddles, to think that I should find you acquainted with the friend of my youth, the companion of earlier days' in that scene in London where, to David's surprise, Mr Micawber 'turns up' in the guise of Tommy Traddles's landlord. The necessity of taking lodgers is, of course, something else the Ivolgins share with the Micawbers, and Madame Ivolgina is no less devoted to her husband than is Mrs Micawber in her more demonstrative way to hers.[12]

Certain other characteristics of the General and of Micawber are also shared by Mr Dorrit. All three continually borrow money: they all go to the debtor's prison, they are all released through the offices of a friend (Myshkin, David, Clennam). The imprisonment of Ivolgin could be matched, in most of its details, from the prison life of either of Dickens's characters:

As for General Ivolgin, a quite unforeseen circumstance occurred at about this time: he was put into the debtor's prison. He was sent there by his friend, the captain's widow, on the basis of recognizances he had given her at various times, amounting in all to two thousand roubles. All this took him completely by surprise, and the poor general was 'decidedly a victim of his unbounded faith, generally speaking, in the generosity of man's heart'. Having acquired the reassuring habit of signing promissory notes and bonds, he did not even entertain the possibility of their having an effect, even at some distant time. He always thought that *that was all.* It turned out that was not all. 'Trust people after that? Show generous trust!' he would sorrowfully exclaim, sitting with his new friends over a bottle of wine in Tarasov's house, and telling them anecdotes about the siege of Kars and the resurrected soldier. Actually he settled in perfectly. Ptitsyn and Varia said it was just the place for him. (pt. II, ch. 1, pp. 212f.)

Oddly enough, General Ivolgin is elected to the chair at the gathering which assembles to celebrate Prince Myshkin's birthday; this must be a reminiscence of the Father of the Marshalsea presiding over the Collegians assembled in the Snuggery for the enjoyment of a 'little Harmony', or of Mr Micawber presiding over the long table at a musical evening in his honour in the King's Bench.

A few other resemblances suggest a relationship between Mr Dorrit and the General in particular, both of whom have gone down in the world and cut themselves off from reality. At one point the General complains to Myshkin of Lebedev's attitude (after Lebedev has started telling him lies almost as extraordinary as his own): 'As for his having some good qualities, I myself was the first to admit it by almost giving this individual [*individuum*] my friendship. . . . But if disrespect should slip through, if maybe this disrespect is a way of showing that the connection is a burden, then an honourable man can only turn away and break off the connection, thus showing the offender his true position.' Mr Dorrit addresses some similar words to his son (on being refused a loan by Mr Clennam): 'Let me suppose the case that I myself may at a certain time – ha – or times, have made a – hum – an appeal, and a properly worded appeal and a delicate appeal, and an urgent appeal, to some individual for a small temporary accommodation. Let me suppose that that accommodation could have been easily extended, and was not extended, and that that individual informed me that he begged to be excused. Am I to be told by my own son, that I therefore received treatment not due to a gentleman, and that I – ha – I submitted to it?'[13] In moments of particularly bad faith, the General's speech becomes almost as jerky as Dorrit's. But above all, the thirteen (or fifteen?)-year-old Kolia Ivolgin looks after his father, and loves him, in something of the manner of Little Dorrit; in one scene we even see him kissing his father's hands. There is no need to balance the claims of Micawber and Dorrit (who, incidentally, were both based on the same man – Dickens's father), but the more interesting influence for the purposes of comparison is the Father of the Marshalsea. In *Little Dorrit* Amy's whole life is built up on love and respect for her father, who inhabits a world of illusion. The problem that confronted Dickens with this self-deceiver was similar to that Dostoevsky faced with the fantastic liar and drunkard, General Ivolgin: how to help a person living in a world of illusion, and what is the right attitude to adopt towards him?

It is a matter of common observation that when Dickens is not enjoying the performances of his characters (as he enjoys Micawber) and their reactions to each other (as he enjoys Clennam's helpless reaction to Flora Finching's garbled picture of happiness) his vision tends to be less free and less true; this is particularly true of characters involved in the plot. With regard to Mr Dorrit, he has a tendency to preach. Sometimes this tendency is no more than a nuisance, as when he heavily underlines a point: 'Thus, now boasting, now despairing, in either fit a captive with the jail-rot upon him, and the impurity of his prison worn into the grain of his soul, he revealed his degenerate state to his affectionate child.' But when his preaching reflects his moral uncertainty and impairs his judgment, it threatens his achievement. Dorrit's devices for cadging 'testimonials' from his visitors are shown in all their embarrassing self-deception but surely there are several things wrong with the prescription for dealing with them that Little Dorrit gives to Clennam:

> Don't encourage him to ask. Don't understand him if he does ask. Don't give it to him. Save him and spare him that, and you will be able to think better of him! . . . You don't know what he is. . . . You don't know what he really is. How can you, seeing him there all at once, dear love, and not gradually as I have done! You have been so good to us, so delicately and truly good, that I want him to be better in your eyes than in anybody's. And I cannot bear to think . . . that you of all the world should see him in his only moments of degradation.

In the first place, to ignore Mr Dorrit's hints is no way of stopping them, as he will only resort to even more obvious and degrading ploys (yet Clennam, who should know better, respects Little Dorrit's appeal). And because of this, there is, in the second place, some uncertainty as to what Little Dorrit means when she speaks of what her father 'really is': the man for whom it was easy to be respectable and decent in the time of prosperity; or a man with human needs and failings who, had he not been corrupted by his prison experiences, might have been a genuinely benevolent father; or the prisoner who depends totally on her for whatever position he has. Her confusion would not be disturbing – Little Dorrit is after all a girl loyally defending her parent – if Dickens did not himself partake of it. It seems that although he aims for the second of these views (he does claim that prison is 'false even with a reference to the falsest condition outside the walls', while his exposure of the pretensions of wealth and snobbery is as thoroughgoing as anything in the book), he in fact tends towards the view that Dorrit should be kept a helpless prisoner. And at times, even in *Little Dorrit*, one cannot avoid feeling that Dickens would prefer not to face human weakness, ugliness, and vice, that he would simply have everyone well-off and respectable.[14]

Consider a parallel situation in *The Idiot*. Within hours of meeting Myshkin, General Ivolgin sends him a message from a café, asking him for an advance of ten roubles.

> Kolia came all the way in and handed the Prince a note. It was from the General, and was folded and sealed. Kolia's face showed how difficult it was for him to hand it over. The Prince read it, stood up, and took his hat.
> 'It's two steps from here', Kolia said embarrassedly. 'He is sitting there over a bottle. What I can't understand is how he got them to give him credit there. Prince . . . [*golubchik*], please don't speak here to my folks about my giving you the note. I've sworn a thousand times not to deliver these notes, but I feel sorry for him. But look, please don't stand on ceremony with him: give him some change, and leave it at that.'

The problem the General presents to his wife is obviously rather greater, but in the words she speaks to the Prince there is a similarly just and subtle understanding:

> 'There is a great deal you will have to excuse Ardalion Aleksandrovich [the General] if you are going to stay with us. However, he will not bother you very much; he even eats alone. You will agree that everybody has his own shortcomings and his own – special characteristics, and that, maybe, this is even truer

of some people than of men who have fingers pointed at them. About one thing, I will make a very special request: if my husband should speak to you about paying the rent for the flat, tell him that you have given it to me. That is, anything you gave to Ardalion Aleksandrovich would of course be entered in your account; it's only because I want to keep things straight that I am asking you.'

Madame Ivolgina and Kolia love the General, as Little Dorrit is supposed to love her father. The person who asks Myshkin not to give the General money is Gania, who cannot stand his father for becoming so disreputable.[15]

The difference between Ivolgin and Dorrit is not that one of them has a complex and interesting psychology while the other has not (as with the Nellies in *The Old Curiosity Shop* and *Insulted and Injured*). Nor is Dickens's uncertain moralizing due to a gap between his perception and his understanding, of the sort we have seen in the preceding chapter in connection with Edith Dombey. Dickens knows Dorrit as well, or almost as well, as Dostoevsky knows Ivolgin. Take the scene where Mr Dorrit breaks down after trying to hint to his daughter that, out of devotion to himself, she should marry the turnkey's son, John Chivery:[16]

> His voice died away, as if she could not bear the pain of hearing him, and her hand had gradually crept to his lips. For a while, there was a dead silence and stillness; and he remained shrunk in his chair, and she remained with her arm around his neck, and her neck bowed down upon his shoulder.
>
> His supper was cooking in a saucepan on the fire, and when she moved, it was to make it ready for him on the table. He took his usual seat, she took hers, and he began his meal. They did not, as yet, look at one another. By little and little he began; laying down his knife and fork with a noise, taking things up sharply, biting at his bread as if he were offended with it, and in other similar ways showing that he was out of sorts. At length he pushed his plate from him, and spoke aloud. With the strangest inconsistency.

Besides being the result of a truly inward knowledge of Mr Dorrit, the moment of silence is superbly rendered thanks to the subsequent stage-business for 'showing that he was out of sorts'; we appreciate here the distinctive strengths Dickens enjoyed through his gifts for acting and producing. But it is unlikely that for Dickens the significance of the scene lies in the silence and stillness. Mr Dorrit afterwards starts to dramatize his situation as a prisoner more and more until, totally blind to its realities, he collapses in his daughter's arms; then, after dramatizing his helplessness as a father, he falls asleep, tended by his daughter. Dickens's explicit comment invites us to see the main purpose of the scene in the tableau of Little Dorrit comforting her father and caring for him in his sleep. 'That child had no doubts, asked herself no questions, for she was but too content to see him with a lustre round his head. Poor dear, good dear, truest, kindest, dearest, were the only words she had for him, as she hushed him to rest.' (p. 231)

There is a comparable scene in which General Ivolgin has a glimpse of his own degradation. He introduces himself to Aglaia, and by way of conversation announces to her, as he does to all young people, that he used to carry her about in his arms. Madame Epanchina promptly accuses him of lying, but by chance the General has in fact been speaking the truth, and Aglaia and her sisters come to his defence, recalling the various things he used to do for them when they were children.

When Aglaia suddenly asserted that he and she had shot a pigeon together, his memory all at once became clear and he remembered it all down to the smallest detail, as something from the distant past is sometimes remembered in one's declining years. It is hard to convey what in this reminiscence was able to act so strongly on the poor and, as was his custom, somewhat drunken General, but he was suddenly unusually moved.

'I remember, I remember everything!' he cried. 'I was a second-captain. You were such a tiny, pretty mite. Nina Aleksandrovna – Gania – I was – received by you, in those days, Ivan Fedorovich –'

'And see what you've come to now!' Madame Epanchina took him up. 'And so you haven't drunk all your good thoughts away, since it's had this effect on you! And how you've worn out your wife. Instead of guiding your children you've been sitting in prison for debt. Go away, old man, go somewhere, stand behind a door in a corner and cry. Remember how innocent you used to be; maybe God will forgive you. Go on, go! I am speaking to you seriously. There is no better way to mend oneself than to think over the past with repentance.'

But it was needless to repeat the serious words. The General, like all constantly drunk people, was very sensitive, and like all inebriates who have sunk too far, could not easily stand memories from the happy past. He stood up, and was walking humbly towards the doors, so that Lizaveta Prokofevna straight away felt sorry for him.

'Ardalion Aleksandrych, old man!' she called after him, 'stop a minute. We're all sinners, and when you feel that your conscience reproaches you less, come to me; we'll sit and talk about the past. You know, maybe I am fifty times worse a sinner than you. Well, goodbye for now, go along, right now there's nothing you –' said she, suddenly growing frightened that he would return.

'Better not go after him for the time being', the Prince stopped Kolia, who was about to run after his father. 'Otherwise he will be vexed, and the whole minute will be spoiled.'

'That's true, don't touch him. Go only in half-an-hour's time', was Lizaveta Prokofevna's pronouncement.

'So that's what it is to speak the truth at any rate once in one's life. It's moved him to tears', Lebedev ventured to insert.

'Well and you must be a fine old man if what I hear is true', Lizaveta Prokofevna at once attacked him. (pt. II, ch. 6, pp. 277f.)

Without asserting that the General's tears are much more than drunken self-pity, Dostoevsky sees that they are a form of self-realization, that if anyone were to go after the General at this moment he would only begin to act out some other part and so hide the truth from himself even further. He is the victim of a personal tragedy. The significance of his moment of truth is further enhanced and generalized by the question Madame Epanchina asks, whether his self-realization is very much less than most of us ever attain.

Part of the reason for Dickens's weakness has to do with Little Dorrit. In her relationship with her father, she does not change and develop, and she never really attempts to understand him. He is, as seen by her, simply a person who needs her love, and she has only one way of showing it. She is, to borrow a useful distinction developed by Robert Garis,[17] a theatrical as opposed to a dramatic character. She demonstrates her love by caring for her father, comforting him, and embracing him (and always in ways that would make it immediately obvious to any spectator that she is a loving daughter). At the same time, since the moral of the whole novel demonstrates the importance of Little Dorrit's goodness, patience, work, and love, there is a danger that her lack of imagination in her relationship with her father will make these virtues seem inadequate. For example, there is the scene in Venice when Mr Dorrit exhorts his daughter to form a surface and reproaches her for continually reminding him of the past. Of course it is wrong of Mr Dorrit to have forgotten the time when he depended on his daughter for everything, but there is something wrong, too, in the way Little Dorrit tries to keep their relationship in its old form: 'She laid her hand on his arm. She did nothing more. She gently touched him. The trembling hand may have said, with some expression, "Think of me, think how I have worked, think of my many cares!" But she said not a syllable herself.' Interestingly, Dickens notes: 'There was a reproach in the touch so addressed to him that she had not foreseen, or she would have withheld her hand.' But Dickens makes nothing of this glimmer of self-awareness (and indeed he allows Little Dorrit to leave her hand on her father's arm during what follows). The scene continues with Mr Dorrit 'running down by jerks', until he falls silent, looks at her (but Dickens makes nothing of this), and ends up in her arms, whimpering that he is 'a poor ruin and a poor wretch in the midst of his wealth'. Little Dorrit seems to make demands on her father – more so than she or Dickens is aware.[18]

After he collapses at Mrs Merdle's dinner-party, and becomes the Father of the Marshalsea once again, Little Dorrit is able to care for him in his last illness, as of old (bk. II, ch. 5). 'They were in jail again, and she tended him, and he had constant need of her, and could not turn without her; and he even told her, sometimes, that he was content to have undergone a great deal for her sake. As to her, she bent over his bed with her quiet face against his, and would have laid down her own life to restore him.' The chapter, as a whole, is a powerful one, and gives expression to one of the important themes of the book: the prison world contained possibilities of love and peace which were missing in the outside world. But the way Little Dorrit reverts to her old role of caring for her father is too simple-minded. She never senses that she can no longer rely on her father, or that she must find a new role for herself, or that she should not want to go back to her old relationship. She does of course live in a world of enforced idleness, so that it would be difficult for her to find a role, but there were other worlds – besides the idle rich one and besides the Marshalsea – of which, here, Dickens betrays no awareness. It is as though, by her very presence, Little Dorrit drives her father further into the world of illusion, then waits for him to break down. From this standpoint, there is even some justification for his uneasiness over his daughter's failure to adjust to her new situation.

Fortunately, Mr Dorrit remains true to himself, despite Dickens's failure to enter into Little Dorrit's imagination or to recognize Mr Dorrit's moments of self-realization. The scenes between father and daughter follow much the same course they might do if she did occasionally burst into tears under the strain of her new situation, or if, on the contrary, she occasionally showed signs of greater awareness. At the same time, Mr Dorrit is quite a complex character, who imposes upon himself and upon others. And this is one of the things particularly relating Ivolgin to Mr Dorrit rather than Mr Micawber. We cannot imagine Mr Micawber having moments of truth in the manner of the former two. His real self is always to be 'waiting for something to turn up'. When something does 'turn up', it threatens his identity, until that triumphant moment of self-realization comes with his denunciation of Uriah Heep, and he is again destitute and free to live in hope. Reasons why Dickens should have understood the master-deceiver Mr Dorrit so well readily suggest themselves. He particularly lends himself to Dickens's theatrical techniques; his self-deception is manifested in his always having to act a part. Dickens, himself an actor and producer (and a great observer), can show Dorrit acting and over-acting all sorts of variations on his principal roles – the distinguished gentleman and the benevolent father – with occasional breakdowns to enable him to switch from one role to another. And General Ivolgin, it will be recognized, is a very similar character, except for his having a rather larger repertory of parts – the old soldier, the maker of history, the raconteur, the head of family.

Because Dickens is so uncritically admiring of his heroine, and because she is so uncritical of herself, he treats that splendid performer Mr Dorrit less charitably than he deserved. Of course, there is a sense in which, because of Mr Dorrit's role in the novel, Dickens was not altogether free to enjoy Mr Dorrit's illusions: inside and outside of prison people build them up and cater to them, and in this way

Dickens suggests society's own values are equally illusory and vulnerable. Here Dickens's comedy is almost savage. Where the failure of charity comes in is with the seeming attempt to get Mr Dorrit back, at any cost, into the prison-world. It would be wrong to make the heroine into a symbolic figure of evil; the ostensible meanings of the book are more interesting than any such hidden significance. Dickens's intention is to preserve what is necessary and true in the Victorian domestic virtues – work, love, and patience – but without the grimness and repression of Victorian life (so richly presented in Bleeding Heart Yard). In the conclusion, Little Dorrit is assigned to Clennam, who has tried to break some of the bonds of society, and to take what steps he can to introduce order and purpose in the small world he inhabits. Clennam's sense that there are some things that can never be changed amounts to a sort of maturity. Society is a real prison in this sense, and affords considerable scope for Little Dorrit's patient virtues. But because Dickens is so confident about what his heroine represents in her relations with her father, the pattern is at times obscured, and Little Dorrit's virtues themselves become a sort of prison.

In *The Idiot* Little Dorrit's part is played by Kolia, whose task is simply to stand by his father, keep him out of the worst sort of trouble, and let him be happy in his own way. There is no attempt to make the General recognize Kolia's or anyone else's love, nor to claim that Kolia can achieve very much. In the end no one can do very much more than the General's wife, who has had to assume responsibility for the family and, having recognized the primacy of its claims, gives the General as large a place in it as she can. When Dostoevsky writes that, in consequence, the General has a 'respect verging on adoration' for Madame Ivolgina,[19] we can believe him, and believe, moreover, that the General's feeling derives from a just intuition of what she is, whereas the tears Mr Dorrit sheds in his daughter's arms seem more like another self-dramatization. Dostoevsky sees his character with greater justice, and it seems he wanted to remove the uncomfortable situation in which Little Dorrit is both child and mother to her father. Naturally enough, neither Kolia nor Madame Ivolgina can in the end save the General from himself.

There is one other facet of the General, which relates him to some of the great comic characters Dickens presented to us to be enjoyed rather than judged. Because his stories and acts are so superb and so well carried off, it is always a temptation to become an audience for them. The General is constantly asserting himself in new and improbable ways, as when he rings at a door he has picked out more or less at random and half-convinces the housekeeper who comes to it that he is an intimate friend of the family; or when he tells Prince Myshkin about his fantastic adventures as Napoleon's page-boy and adviser during the occupation of Moscow. He shares a trick with Mrs Gamp and invents a friend, Kapiton Eropegov, to bolster his identity. His lying is so compelling and entertaining that it is impossible to stop him, as even Prince Myshkin finds. And as an outsider, there is nothing the Prince can do for the General, except to pay his debts. Dostoevsky does one thing here that Dickens does not succeed in doing: he takes both views of the General – that of the General's family, for whom he is a serious problem, and that of the outsider, who can see his humorous side – and shows that both are, in a sense, justified.[20] It is doubtful that this achievement of Dostoevsky's would have been possible without Little Dorrit's moralistic outlook or her father's performances. Ivolgin is the most intractably human of the characters in *The Idiot*. Through him Dostoevsky's daemonic universe relates most directly to the everyday world which limits our thoughts.

Notes

1 Prince Myshkin in *The Idiot*, pt. I, ch. 5, p. 68 (in *Sobranie sochinenii*, vol. 6).
2 *Little Dorrit*, bk. I, ch. 10, pp. 104f.
3 *The Idiot*, pt. III, ch. 1, p. 368.
4 *Little Dorrit*, bk. II, ch. 28, p. 749; *The Idiot*, pt. I, ch. 10, p. 132.
5 *Little Dorrit*, bk. I, ch. 13, p. 160; *The Idiot*, pt. III, ch. 4, pp. 423f.
6 *F. M. Dostoevsky: Materialy i issledovaniia*, ed. A. S. Dolinin (Leningrad, 1936, p. 524).
7 No. 302, *Pis'ma*, vol. 2. Note the shift from the need for practical men to the need for Russian men. The call for guns was a response to Napoleon III.
8 *Little Dorrit*, bk. I, ch. 2, p. 18; ch. 10, p. 119.
9 See *The Idiot*, pt. IV, ch. 6, p. 593.
10 Pt. III, ch. 4, pp. 422–30.
11 *The Hero in Eclipse in Victorian Fiction* (Oxford, 1956), p. 388.
12 *Copperfield*, ch. 27, pp. 406f.; *The Idiot*, pt. I, ch. 8, p. 109.
13 *Little Dorrit*, bk. I, ch. 31, p. 376; *The Idiot*, pt. IV, ch. 4, pp. 559f. Dorrit's change of tack in his peroration is Dostoevsky performed by the Inimitable Boz: 'If you are not filial, sir, if you discard that duty, you are at least – hum – not a Christian? Are you – ha – an Atheist? And is it Christian, let me ask you, to stigmatize and denounce an individual for begging to be excused this time, when the same individual may – ha – respond with the

required accommodation next time? Is it the part of a Christian not to –
hum –'not to try again?'

14 *Little Dorrit*, bk. I, ch. 7, p. 71; ch. 14, pp. 171f.; ch. 19, p. 229.
15 *The Idiot*, pt. I, ch. 8, pp. 113f.; ch. 11, pp. 142, 145.
16 *Little Dorrit*, bk. I, ch. 19, p. 227.
17 *The Dickens Theatre* (Oxford, 1965).
18 *Little Dorrit*, bk. II, ch. 5, pp. 479f.
19 Pt. IV, ch. 3, pp. 545f.
20 The one person in the prison-world who might have been equipped to
     share Dickens's own savagely humorous view of Mr Dorrit is Pancks.

6

The Devils:
disintegration

The Dostoevskys were living in Dresden when, in October 1869, Anna's brother came on a visit to them from Moscow, where he attended the Petrovskaia Agricultural Academy. His friends among the students there included one Ivanov, who had belonged to a revolutionary cell but broke away following a quarrel with its founder and leader, Nechaev. On 25 November Ivanov's body was found in a pond in the grounds of the Academy. It came out that he had been murdered by Nechaev and some members of the cell. Upon reading the story in the papers, Dostoevsky was disturbed and amazed, seeing in it a subject for a novel.[1] He was already at work on an ambitious project he had conceived – a series of linked novels under the general title of 'The Life of a Great Sinner', having for hero a man of Dostoevsky's generation who was to spend his life wavering between atheism and faith. The novel about the Nechaev affair was supposed to be short and easy to write; it would be finished by the autumn of 1870, leaving Dostoevsky free to tackle his larger project. 'For the thing I am writing for *Russkii vestnik* I have strong hopes, not for its artistic but for its tendentious side; I want to get a few ideas off my mind even if my artistry has to perish. But I am carried away by what has been building up in my mind and heart; even if it comes out as a pamphlet, I'll say my piece.'[2] In the event, Dostoevsky's work on his 'pamphlet' was to continue until the end of 1872.

A letter of 9/21 October 1870 to N. N. Strakov mentions the difficulties Dostoevsky met in the early stages of composition:

> In a word, nothing has ever given me so much work. At first, that is to say the end of last year, I looked at it as something that was extorted and factitious; I looked down on it. Then real

inspiration visited me – and I suddenly began to love it, and went at it with both hands – and, so, crossed out what I had written. Then in the summer months another . . . change: a new person emerged with claims to be the real *hero of the novel*, so that the previous hero (a curious person, but who does not deserve the name of hero) moved out of the foreground [*stal na vtoroi plan*]. The new hero so captivated me that again I began a new version. (no. 358, *Pis'ma*, vol. 2)

The picture revealed by the notebooks[3] is even more complicated. At first a prominent role was to be played by a character based on a real person (Golubov) who had left the Old Believers to join the Orthodox Church, and whose ideas attracted Dostoevsky. He was meant to appear as the teacher of 'Ivanov' (Shatov); 'the prince' (Stavrogin) as well came under his influence, while even 'Nechaev' (Peter Verkhovensky) had to contend with him. But simultaneously Dostoevsky was working on 'The Life of a Great Sinner', and seems to have had difficulty in keeping the material for the two novels separate; Stavrogin grew in importance. When Dostoevsky finally decided to eliminate Golubov (on 29 March [O.S.] 1870), Stavrogin was designated the principal hero. His pre-eminence, however, was not yet secure; a letter dated 8/20 October suggests that in the draft produced in the spring and early summer of 1870, the 'curious person' who was the original hero was probably Peter Verkhovensky. Stavrogin became the key figure only in the final draft.

> One of the major events in my story will be the well-known murder of Ivanov by Nechaev in Moscow. I hasten to specify: I knew neither Nechaev, nor Ivanov, nor the circumstances of the murder, and do not know them at all except from newspapers. And even if I did, I could not copy. I am taking only the accomplished fact. My fantasy may differ in very great measure from the actual reality and my Peter Verkhovensky may in no way resemble Nechaev; but it seems to me that, in my astounded mind, my imagination has created the person or type corresponding to this wicked deed. No doubt, it is not without use to present such a man, but on his own he would not tempt me. In my opinion these pitiful monstrosities are not worthy of literature. To my own surprise this person is turning out half-comic in my novel. And therefore even though the whole event

is enacted in one of the foregrounds of the novel, it is, nonetheless, only an accessory and a setting for the actions of another person who could indeed be called the principal person in the novel.

This other person (Nicholas Stavrogin) is also dark and wicked. Yet it seems to me this character is tragic, even though in reading many will ask, What is this? I am sitting down to write a poem about this person because I have been wanting to depict [*izobrazit'*] him for too long. In my opinion he is both Russian and typical. I shall be very very sad if he does not succeed. I shall be even sadder if the verdict I hear is that he is stilted. I have taken him from my heart. Of course this is a character rarely appearing in all its typicality, but it is a Russian one (from a certain layer of society). (no. 356, *Pis'ma*, vol. 2)

When the first chapters were complete, Stavrogin was intended as a tragic figure. But his vicissitudes were not ended. Dostoevsky wanted to have him visit a saintly monk, Tikhon, and show him a written confession of a rape committed upon a young girl, who had subsequently killed herself. The editor of *Russkii vestnik* refused to publish Stavrogin's confession, and turned down a second version of it in which the rape could be seen as an imaginary one. Dostoevsky interrupted his work for several months. On returning to it he apparently gave up any thought of using the confession or even of inserting it when the novel appeared in a separate edition. Thus the earlier portion of *The Devils* was written for a Stavrogin which included a meeting with Tikhon, and the latter portion for a Stavrogin whose role did not include such a meeting.

The essential unity of the novel did not necessarily suffer. There is good evidence[4] that, from the start, Dostoevsky had been hesitating between two conceptions of Stavrogin and was trying to keep both options open: one in which Stavrogin met a 'tragic' end after trying to achieve a spiritual rebirth; the other in which he was such a degenerate that he could only come to an 'ignoble' end. Each of the two versions of the 'Confession' reflects a different one of the conceptions. Dostoevsky's decision was in effect made for him by the refusal of *Ruskii vestnik* to publish the chapter, leaving him with the 'ignoble' Stavrogin. None the less, whether because Dostoevsky really was confused, or because his intentions were frustrated, or for some other reason, critics account for Stavrogin's role in contradictory ways. According to Mochulsky, *The Devils* was going to be a diptych opposing the Christian ideal to an image of hell and destruction, except that the omission of Stavrogin's visit to Tikhon deprived the diptych of one of its leaves; hence *The Devils* is principally about the Satanic figure of Nicholas Stavrogin, who is the source of chaos, and the revolutionary activities are peripheral to him. But according to Ernest Simmons, Stavrogin really belongs to the romantic part of the story and the revolutionary plot is something separate, with which he is not effectively integrated. Another frequent suggestion is that Stavrogin acts the part of the man from whom a legion of devils is expelled, as in the story of the Gadarene swine.

Obviously these interpretations are not all compatible. In view of all the disagreement over Stavrogin's role, it might appear there was good reason for George Katkov's claim that the concealed ties 'which connect this mysterious character with the complicated mechanism of the plot' are so difficult to uncover because Dostoevsky was working under the influence of Dickens's character, Steerforth.[5] Of course, if this is correct, it appears that Stavrogin was a private symbol, whose significance Dostoevsky did not elucidate. Katkov's whole argument rests on his assumption (p. 485) that in *The Devils* Dostoevsky was seeking to account for a 'monstrous' murder which he identified with the 'problem of the origin of an autonomous will for evil in man', and on the perfectly (much too perfectly) matched assumption (p. 486) that he had a special desire to deduce revolutionary movements from the 'mentality of the daemonic rebel'. (Doesn't this amount to saying that an evil deed can be done only by a man who can do an evil deed?) Nechaev-Verkhovensky seemed so insignificant a figure of evil that Dostoevsky was led to introduce as the real culprit one of 'the artificial types derived from the sublime Marquis' – Steerforth. Stavrogin was Steerforth done over by Dostoevsky. But in what sense is Stavrogin the real culprit? To the extent that Katkov's procedure is not circular, it is mere assertion. Although his assumptions could be challenged, it is much more profitable to consider again whether a satisfactory account really cannot be given of the novel and of Stavrogin's part in it, and then to take another look at this character's relationship to Steerforth. Fortunately our freedom to suggest interpretations has some limits put on it by Dostoevsky's own words in a letter of 9/21 October 1870 to Maikov (no. 357, *Pis'ma*, vol. 2):

the illness which has taken possession of civilized Russians is much stronger than we imagined. . . the devils have come out of Russian man and entered a herd of swine, i.e. the Nechaevs, Serno-Soloveviches etc. These have drowned or will surely drown, while the healed man, out of whom the devils have come, is sitting at Jesus' feet. . . . . Russia has spewed forth this filth with which she was stuffed, and of course there remained nothing Russian in the scoundrels she has spewed.

In other words, the devils were supposed to come out of civilized Russia. This conception holds good in the completed novel; on his deathbed Stepan Trofimovich has a vision of Russia healed and sitting at Christ's feet. Any account of the novel as a whole must allow for this vision of the country's fate.

Interpretation and structure

Dostoevsky's imagination worked dramatically; his novels form dynamic wholes. And because his characters are genuinely free – with a range of choices open to them – it is plausible to suggest that Dostoevsky could overcome even so great a disaster as the cancellation of the 'Confession'. In 'A Contemporary Falsehood',[6] one year after completing *The Devils*, Dostoevsky described his purpose in writing it: 'My Nechaev is of course, unlike the real person. I wanted to ask a question and give the clearest possible answer to it in the form of a novel; how is it that – in our transitional and amazing modern society – not Nechaev, but *Nechaevs* are possible, and how can it come about that these *Nechaevs* eventually gather Nechaev-ites around them?' Dostoevsky still regarded the Nechaev-problem as central to his novel, even though Peter Verkhovensky had turned out not to be the hero. But the problem was now presented in much more general terms. Men like Verkhovensky could have a real influence, and that was what needed to be explained. Revolution was a serious matter for Dostoevsky; as a member of the Petrashevsky circle, he himself had in effect been, as he goes on to say, a Nechaev-ite, although he probably could not have been another Nechaev. His article shows that, in explaining the existence of Nechaev-type revolutionaries, he was trying to understand a social situation: 'The horror is that here a man can do an utterly vile and filthy deed without having to be in any way a scoundrel! This is not the case here alone, but has always been so, all over the world, from the earliest ages, in times of transition and convulsion in men's lives, times of doubt and denial, of scepticism and shakiness [*shatost'*] in the fundamental convictions of society.' From the start Dostoevsky was concerned with the causes and nature of disintegration.

In his novel as in the article, Dostoevsky is protesting about the failure of his fellow Russians to recognize the most obvious truths about their country – a concern illustrated in his handling of the workers' demonstration which takes place on the day before the fête. The townspeople totally misunderstand its significance, see it as a rebellion and look for a political motive behind it. Dostoevsky insists on doing the workers justice: it was natural for them to protest to the governor for a redress of their wrongs; this was a traditional form of protest which had nothing to do with the leaflets distributed by the revolutionaries. He makes fun of the tendency of the townspeople to find easy solutions and easy ways of salving their conscience. In their stories about the disturbances, they even go so far as to invent a victim, Avdotia Petrovna Tarapygina, who springs to life as a figure of local and even national fame:[7]

> Many of our people spoke about some woman from the cemetery almshouse, Avdotia Petrovna Tarapygina, claiming that, as she had been passing through the square on her way back to the almshouse after a visit to some friends, she had, it seemed, pushed her way through the spectators, out of natural curiosity, and seeing what was going on, cried out, 'What a disgrace!' and spat. For this she was, supposedly, seized and 'dealt with'. Not only was this incident published in the papers, but in the heat of the moment a subscription was raised for her in the town. I myself subscribed twenty kopecks. And now what? It turns out there was no such almshouse Tarapygina in our town at all. I went myself to inquire in the almshouse by the cemetery: they had never heard of any Tarapygina there, and, moreover, were very offended when I told them the rumour that was going about.

The questions to consider about this society are what is its moral condition, and what lays it open to revolutionary influences. One 'fact' provides the framework of the novel: God is the foundation of the whole moral edifice; without him everything goes. The anonymous captain who exclaims 'If there is no God, what kind of captain am I?' gives expression to this basic premiss. Shatov expounds it when he says that each people has its own god, whether it be Nature as with the Greeks, or the Roman concept of government, or the Christian God cherished by the Russians; and that a nation begins to die out and to lose its sense of good and evil the moment it starts sharing its gods.[8] The whole novel can be seen as an examination of this premiss, and at the same time, as an attempt to find a new god and so to safeguard a distinction between good and evil.

The liberals as represented by Stephan Trofimovich Verkhovensky and his friends have long since lost their faith in the Russian God. The revolutionaries, in concert with the group surrounding the governor's wife, Madame von Lembke, now seize upon every opportunity of discrediting religious belief. The peasants are ready to turn back to their own, more primitive gods. And Peter Verkhovensky understands the situation better than anyone:

'Listen, first trouble will be unleashed by us', Verkhovensky spoke in a terrible hurry, continually clutching Stavrogin by the left sleeve. 'I have already told you, we will get right inside the people. Do you know, even now we are terribly strong? Our men are not only the ones who cut throats and burn or do a classical shot or bite one another. Those are only in the way. I understand nothing without discipline. You see, I am a scoundrel and not a socialist, ha ha! Listen, I have counted them all: the teacher laughing with his pupils about their God and their cradle is already ours. The advocate pleading that an educated murderer was more highly developed than his victims, and so was bound to kill for the sake of money, is already ours. Schoolboys killing a peasant for the feel of it – ours. . . . The administrators, the literary men, oh, there are lots of us, and they themselves do not know it. . . . The Russian God has already capitulated to cheap booze. The people are drunk, the mothers drunk, the children drunk, the churches empty. . . . Oh, let this generation grow up. A pity, though, there's no time to wait, else they could grow drunker! Pshaw, what a pity there're no proletarians! But there will be, there will, it's coming.' (pt. II, ch. 8, pp. 439f.)

Peter Verkhovensky knows that without a myth to which men can relate their feelings and aspirations no concerted action is possible. The revolutionaries do not escape this general rule, as we see at the meeting of radicals at Virginsky's house (for which Dostoevsky could draw on his own reminiscences). These crude de-mythologizers ('We know, for example, that the superstition about God began with thunder and lightning') have put themselves in Verkhovensky's hands.

The place of Stepan Trofimovich in the total structure is plain. The account of his group of 'free-thinkers' and of his relations with his patroness, at the opening of the novel, is rich with the sense of arrested time and decay. He is a man of the Forties, and along with the other men of his generation, with their ideas deriving from the Utopian Socialists and the German Idealists, has helped to dislodge the national God, and to hold up instead some sort of abstract Deity or (it is not always clear which) Hegelian Absolute Being. The radicals of the Sixties who threaten society with actual disintegration have simply taken some of these ideas about God and Russia a little further, and use them as a basis for action. Significantly, most of the men in Stepan Trofimovich's circle join the revolutionary cell when it is set up. The link between the generations is cemented by Stepan Trofimovich's relationships with two of the characters on whom the action of the novel chiefly rests – his son, Peter Verkhovensky, and his pupil, Nicholas Stavrogin. The son, whom out of carelessness he abandoned in child-hood, has grown up to be a revolutionary. Meanwhile the noble ideas of old Verkhovensky have excited insatiable longings in Stavrogin (pt. I, ch. 2, i): '. . . the friends used to weep and fling their arms around each other at night, and not always because of a little domestic scene. Stepan Trofimovich succeeded in sounding some of the deepest chords in his friend's heart and in arousing in him the first, still indefinite sensation of that ever-lasting and sacred sorrow which, once tasted and known by an elect spirit, will never be exchanged for cheap satis-faction.' In the adult Stavrogin, romantic nostalgia turns into Byronic craving for stimulation.

The Byronism which Stavrogin exhibits can certainly appeal to any liking we have for the sensational: the question is whether it has any further significance. His attributes include rebelliousness, fascination, a sense of ennui and superiority, an aura of unspeakable crimes; and he leads a strangely spectacular and inconsequent life made up of brilliant social successes in St Petersburg, slumming, travels in Egypt and to Jerusalem and Iceland, and studies at a German university. He kills an adversary in a duel; pulls an old clubman across a room by the nose; bites a provincial governor's ear. On one of his visits home the provincial ladies expect him to be a sort of vampire; instead he turns out to be a 'gentleman in fashion-plate'. Everyone's attention is fastened on him, his life in the capital and abroad is a constant subject of gossip. When the novel opens there is an atmosphere of suspense. Several of his associates have turned up, his own arrival is imminent and anxiously awaited. When at last he walks into his mother's house one Sunday on which, through one of Dostoevsky's great contrivances, the key figures in Stavrogin's story are almost all assembled, his behaviour lives up to every expectation. He acknowledges a special relationship between himself and the crippled, feeble-witted Maria Lebiadkina, yet mysteriously avoids answering the question whether or not he is married to her. Then Shatov walks up to him and strikes him, and Stavrogin, for all his notorious ruthlessness, does not retaliate. Not surprisingly, his apparent cowardice generates all sorts of scurrilous gossip, until suddenly he is set forth in a new light thanks to a few words spoken in public by the governor's wife.[9] His acceptance of Shatov's slap in the face is a sign that he has found a code of behaviour adopted to the changed times; he could not challenge a former serf of his to a duel, and 'scorned the opinion of a society which had not grown into the right sense of things'. As a 'new man' who is also an 'undoubted nobleman' and the greatest landlord in the province, he is destined to be one of society's leaders.

The attitude of the provincial town is, I think, suggestive. Stavrogin is a fitting leader – though not quite in the way people think. He is ahead of other men in feeling that good and evil no longer bear any real relation to conduct and that God is dead; he is not so far ahead that he cannot participate in some, at any rate, of the escapades of Madame von Lembke and her ladies. The language and thoughts of men have lost all real meaning for him; hence he is constantly trying new roles. When old Gaganov exclaims to a group of men in the club that he'll not be led by the nose, Stavrogin proves to him that he literally shall be led by the nose. His reasons for marrying Maria Lebiadkina are, in part, a 'need for moral sensuality' and a 'passion for torture' (at any rate according to Shatov, and Stavrogin does not deny the charge).[10] He likes to challenge his own powers of sanity. But if he is far more restlessly probing than anyone else in the stagnating society of *The Devils*, none the less his exploration of ideas and behaviour is particularly significant because it is a search conducted by a member of *that* society.

In the 'Night' chapters at the beginning of Part II, in the course of which Stavrogin calls on and has long talks with Peter Verkhovensky, Kirillov, Shatov, and Maria Lebiadkina and her brother, we can recognize that his behaviour has been, among other things, a search for a god and a myth (this is what makes him Satanic). There is a change of mood; the individuated narrator disappears. Stavrogin is confronted again with ideas he has contemplated in the past. Kirillov wants to show that man is free, and believes that to do this he must prove that man is God, and himself become the Christ-figure who will reveal the new religion. Shatov wants to find the Christian God – a new or at any rate unknown One – harboured by the Russian people. Maria Lebiadkina, Stavrogin's wife, speaks for a barely Christianized and still animistic Russia – the Mother Earth which men have wounded. Even the buffoonlike Captain Lebiadkin, her brother, has the makings of a strictly utilitarian myth to offer; he thinks of imitating the American millionaire who wanted his skin to be made into a drum on which to beat out the national anthem day and night. Peter Verkhovensky's revolutionary myth is not revealed until later, after the state of society has been more fully explored.

In the end the alternative myths fail. Kirillov's failure is perhaps inevitable. He wants to kill himself for the sake of man, yet the 'rather indifferent' tone of voice in which he speaks to Stavrogin of his liking for children, his lack of friends, and even his description of the yellowing leaf – all suggest a limited capacity for loving man and life. There is something revealing in his belief that all men are good, and that they need only recognize this fact in order to be good. Stavrogin demonstrates the vacuity of this reasoning by retorting: 'If you knew that you believed in God you would believe, but since you do not know that you believe in God you do not believe.' Kirillov rejects this as a display of wit (yet learns enough from it to find the key to Stavrogin's character: 'If Stavrogin believes, then he does not believe that he believes; if he does not believe, then he does not believe that he does not believe.') Kirillov is relying on words to give the answer to life: 'All my life I have wanted it not to be mere words. I lived because I didn't want that.' Even though in some of his last speeches he seems to go beyond words and to lay the foundations of a new religion based on the myth of the man-god, we do not expect him to succeed in conquering his own fear of death. The description of his suicide – with his terrible cries 'Now, now, now, now' – suggests that he conquers neither fear nor time.[11]

Maria Lebiadkina and Shatov must die because their myths are less powerful than Peter Verkhovensky's. The intellectually and physically maimed Maria Lebiadkina does not stand a chance. Her image is beautifully drawn; still there is something too essentially mindless about her, something primeval about her identification with nature and mother-earth. She belongs to the primitive world of folklore conjured up by Peter Verkhovensky (in 'Ivan-the-Tsarevich'). It is with Shatov's death that Dostoevsky comes closest to creating a sense of the loss threatened through the disintegration of society. On the night before Shatov is to die, his wife, Marie, returns to him and gives birth to another man's child (Stavrogin's). From a gloomy, brooding theorizer, Shatov is transformed into a man having a living relation with another being. The sensual and emotional self in him is released – we feel this in the furious energy with which he pounds on the shutters at the mid-wife's house – and is acknowledged by his wife when the baby is delivered (pt. III, ch. 5): 'suddenly her left arm quickly embraced his neck, and on his forehead he felt her firm, moist kiss.' In Dostoevsky's novel this stands out as an unusually direct rendering of sensuous experience. The flow of emotion is cathartic; Shatov is able to speak to Kirillov, with whom he has scarcely exchanged a word since the time in America when they both spent three months lying side-by-side sick with fever. Marie and the midwife attending her are representative of the emancipated women that are hastening the collapse of society (yet Marie's every moment is an acknowledgment of the wrong she has done her husband); and so overriding is Shatov's joyful celebration of new life that it seems to carry everything with it.

In a time of disintegration there is no place for the mystery of birth. Shortly after Marie's return, Erkel, a revolutionary, calls on Shatov to arrange the meeting at which he is supposed to sever his links with the group. To identify himself, Erkel describes a sign in Shatov's hand; it is a reminder of the secret horror of Peter Verkhovensky's organization (throughout it is associated with cannibals and with vermin). Before, we were entitled to feel that the whole society deserved to disappear; now, thanks to Shatov, a sense of value is created. Because of what he has become, the cry of one of the revolutionaries, 'It's not that, not that! No not that at all!' after Shatov lies murdered, has something of the force of a moment of insight and self-knowledge in a tragedy.

As for Stavrogin, he has found that no myth has any power over him. He is too aware of the defects in Shatov's and Kirillov's arguments to take the search for a Russian God or a man-god seriously (of course, he himself first suggested their theories to them). And because his capacity for feeling is atrophied, he could never sense the beauty of Maria Lebiadkina's intuition that 'the great moist earth' is the Mother of God (and hence the source of all value). His inability to feel deeply or sustainedly about anything undermines even his resolutions to behave like a decent man; he assumes responsibility for the lives of Shatov and Maria Lebiadkina, but fails to live up to it and, so, brings about not only their deaths but his own son's. He has no real duty to Russia past, present, or future. He dies a citizen of the canton of Uri – as much as to say, a citizen of nowhere. About him and the whole society for which he stands, there is, in the end, nothing to be said. In the description of his death which closes the novel, no deep emotions are stirred, only a rather dry disgust. The last letter he writes to Dasha, besides reviewing his whole life, suggests that he has killed himself out of indifference – because good and evil have ceased to exist for him. Kirillov held that man would be free only when it was a matter of indifference to live or not to live; Stavrogin shows what this freedom amounts to, and we recognize at the same time that the myth of the man-god was stillborn.[12] Although he will not help Peter Verkhovensky to harness the forces of darkness and establish a despotic power, he has allowed himself to be associated, by default, with the aims of that revolutionary.

Dostoevsky's novel is about disintegration. The failure of the life-asserting myths – Shatov's, Kirillov's, and Maria Lebiadkina's – reinforces our sense that there was no easy way out for Stavrogin's society. There was nothing to take the place of the dying God. The basic pattern of the novel is, on one level, an exploration of the death-pangs of the old God and the old morality and, on another, a search for a new god (Verkhovensky's place in the scheme will be considered later). Here and there the pattern is blurred. Kirillov's ideas, tone of voice, fate, and actions are in constant relation with one another, and something about his way of speaking – in short, choppy sentences – suggests that his man-god is a mere logical construct. But why is he an engineer? And it is implausible to suggest that he would sign a letter confessing to the murder of Shatov; he would surely realize that in acknowledging an obligation to do this he makes a farce of his theory. With Shatov, too, there is a problem: how should we take the scenes in which he welcomes his wife and her child? It is true that he is meant to have a reverence for life wherever it is found (and at one point, he defends his use of a certain expression, saying 'It is in the spirit of the language'). But he is also a Slavophile who holds that a nation must be convinced of its superiority, and a fanatic tortured by his inability to accept God. The rendering of experience is so first-hand when he is reunited with Marie that it might seem he has finally escaped from the theory crushing him. Or perhaps the birth is vindication and a transcendence of the theory: there is a feeling of ritual, a Christmas with a terrible new beauty is celebrated. The birth seems to have some larger meaning, and might be connected with the God Shatov has been so desperately looking for. Because the relationship between theory and sacrament is not fully brought out, the Slavophile killed by Peter Verkhovensky receives more sympathy than he deserves. The main conception of the novel, however, is unaffected.

The sort of situation in which a man like Nechaev could have an influence was, as Dostoevsky's novel so fully shows, a time of moral and spiritual collapse. The stress is not on economic and social analysis; if anything Dostoevsky's insight is more like an anthropologist's. As he works out the plot, it becomes a means of exploring a society in danger of disintegration, and for which there is no salvation. It is a nation that has lost the will to live, and has reached a point where economic and social reforms would be meaningless. While evil could never be eradicated, in some societies it could acquire enormous power. Because the society Peter Verkhovensky operates in has lost any strong sense of good and evil, even decent men and women can work with him and make themselves the unwitting agents of their own destruction. What the Stavrogin parts of the novel show is the importance of myth for the individual, for a movement, and for society. A primitive, demoniac, destructive myth could give Russians a sense of energy and purpose. The Orthodox God they had shoved aside was as powerless to do that for them as the shallow-rooted European civilization they had imported.

In 1877 Dostoevsky wrote:[13]

a huge portion of the Russian order of life has remained utterly without observation and without a *historian*. At any rate, it is clear that the life of our upper-middle gentry, so vividly described by our belles-lettrists, is by now too insignificant and specialized a corner of Russian life. Who then will be the *historian* of the remaining corners, of which, it seems, there are so frightfully many? And if in this chaos – in which our social life has long been and is especially so nowadays – it is still impossible even perhaps for an artist of Shakespearian dimensions to seek out a normal law and a guiding thread, then, at the very least, who will illuminate just part of the chaos even if it's done without thought of a guiding thread? The main thing is it seems nobody is at all up to it yet; it seems premature even for our greatest artists. Without question, we have a disintegrating life and consequently a disintegrating family. But we have the essentials and a life forming itself anew on new foundations. Who will discern them, and who will point them out? Who can in the least little bit define and express the laws of this disintegration and new construction? Or is it still too early?

Dostoevsky is the artist-historian who sees and tries to explain the breakdown of the old order and looks for the new emerging order. His concern with society is reflected in the structure of his novels. His originality of form is a measure of his understanding. Dostoevsky says in the notebooks for *The Devils* that Shakespeare embodies not only the everyday reality, but that part of reality which is 'contained in the form of the still hidden, unexpressed future Word'.[14] In this Dostoevsky is, with Shakespeare, a prophet.

Steerforth and Stavrogin

So far as the structure of *The Devils* is concerned, Stavrogin's role is to act out other men's dreams and fantasies, ask the questions they cannot put in words, and give shape and meaning to the chaos they live in. His mission is messianic. But behind his mysterious mask lies a void; he is a usurper. The interesting question for criticism is his role rather than his character. If his 'Confession' to Tikhon had been included, the added psychological drama would have obscured his role; the elimination of the 'Confession' (which Dostoevsky regarded as permanent) has resulted in a tidier – and better – novel. If this interpretation of *The Devils* is correct, Steerforth is hardly needed to tell us about Stavrogin's mysterious relationship with the plot. Nevertheless

Katkov's view that Stavrogin derives from Steerforth is, I think, correct. His claim has been quietly accepted or else ignored – but not disputed. It might have excited greater interest had Katkov presented a clear argument. His confusions of method and literary analysis are reflected in his description of the parallels. A good example is provided by his statement (p. 474) that both characters 'become the inspiring factor for the actions of others, which they themselves do not intend to inspire and for which they are unwilling to assume responsibility'. Whether or not the former part of the statement applies to Steerforth, the latter part certainly does not apply to Stavrogin, who is hardly unwilling to assume responsibility for Maria Lebiadkina and Shatov (although he fails to live up to it). But it can be seen why Katkov should want to make this claim; it enables him to assert (p. 486) that Stavrogin was 'basically responsible for all the series of crimes' although he was 'so little implicated in them that he could easily be omitted from a purely causal explanation'. An inadequate critical view of Dostoevsky's novel (and of Dickens's) distorts Katkov's findings.

There are other radical confusions in Katkov. He thinks that if Steerforth is Stavrogin's prototype this knowledge will help us to understand Stavrogin's role and significance, and then shows that in Stavrogin the 'autonomous will for evil' is in fact much more unambiguous than in Dickens's character. But if this is so, then surely the latter is an even greater mystery than Dostoevsky's figure and is no help to us. Furthermore, Katkov seems to think that Stavrogin is simply Steerforth done over by Dostoevsky; thus he builds too much on to individual parallels, and they begin to break down when he sees parody in one place and a heightening of tragic tension in another. And Katkov's view of tragedy is deficient; for anything he says, Dostoevsky might simply have stripped Dickens's Byronic hero of a role from the melodramatic repertoire (the seduction of Little Emily) and at the same time of a plausible and, in context, interesting class outlook, in order to restore him as a Romantic Rebel cloaked in satanic mystery. The gain is not obvious. Because of the confusion in Katkov's mind he is trapped in a maze of circular and illusory explanations.

The important parallels to which Katkov has directed us can be briefly set forth. Both Steerforth and Stavrogin are characterized by Byronic pride and self-will, egotism, sense of superiority, and the many roles they act. They are engaged in a restless search for strange new experiences and people (note that Stavrogin speaks of a visit to

Tikhon as an opportunity to become acquainted with 'that sort of people' – the same terms Steerforth uses when David suggests he come to Yarmouth to see the Peggottys). Their charm is a cover for emotional coldness, while their moral sense has withered, leaving them only with a vestigial longing to do good (their warped development is associated with their lack of a father). They are natural leaders, who attract weaker men, and can get away with insulting and betraying their friends (in particular David and Shatov). In the end they are disowned by their mothers, who are as proud and self-willed as the sons.

Dostoevsky's novel bears the imprint of those strange scenes in that house at Highgate inhabited by two women frozen in rigid stances – Mrs Steerforth, with her confidence in the superior destiny cut out for her son, and her ward Rosa Dartle, always waiting for the moment when the tensions between mother and son will erupt. In *The Devils* (pt. I, ch. 5) Stavrogin comes home to confront his mother, whose attitude is sometimes one of proud identification with her son, and sometimes one of fearful anticipation. She, too, has a ward, Dasha, who knows Stavrogin as well as Rosa Dartle knows Steerforth. On his last visit home Steerforth is 'particularly attentive and respectful' to his mother. Stavrogin, when challenged by his mother to declare whether he is married to the lame and simple-minded Maria Lebiadkina, goes over to his mother and kisses her hand with respect, and then addresses Maria in a 'kind and melodious voice', with a look of 'unusual tenderness' (Steerforth has won Little Emily's confidence with his gentle and respectful manner). The appeal which Captain Lebiadkin makes in the name of his sister to Madame Stavrogina could have been suggested by the one Mr Peggotty makes to Mrs Steerforth. It is perhaps significant that Little Emily has always wanted to be a lady, and that Maria Lebiadkina (pt. II, ch. 2, ii) is troubled by the difficulties of being a countess. And as Katkov suggests, the scene (pt. II, ch. 1, iv) in which Stavrogin's mother enters his study and finds him asleep 'resembling an inanimate wax figure' looks like an amalgam of three images: the repeated descriptions of Steerforth asleep in his accustomed position; the picture of him lying dead on the beach in the same position; and the description of his bedroom, in which hangs a portrait of his mother, 'as if it were even something to her that her likeness should watch him while he slept'. The views of Steerforth asleep serve of course as a warning signal, but they also have the force of a poetic image, capturing something of the contradiction between

Steerforth's seeming beauty and the strange things he actually does. This contradiction is also characteristic of Stavrogin.[15]

Passion and violence are other links between the characters. The scar on Rosa Dartle's face is, Katkov thinks, a 'conventional symbol for some kind of sexual aggression committed by Steerforth', in consequence of which she has been left with an erotic fixation on him. Certainly the erotic fixation is plain enough, and while it is Liza who has the really erotic fixation on Stavrogin, there are hints of a sexual liaison between him and Dasha (and Dasha's love for him is slavelike, as is Rosa's for Steerforth). It is difficult to tell from the drafts, but it is possible that some of the earlier versions of Stavrogin's character were also shaped by the influence (Katkov assumes without warrant that it was dominant throughout). In the early plans of Dostoevsky's novel the hero assaults the 'Teacher'; even though the notebooks will hardly show that this attack derives from Steerforth's insulting of Mr Mell, it is odd that Shatov (who eventually emerges from the Teacher) accuses Stavrogin of corrupting Kirillov's mind, and that Mr Mell levels a similar charge against Steerforth.

What is crucial to Steerforth is David's admiration for him. After the abduction of Little Emily, David Copperfield gives a remarkable testimony to his affection for his friend: 'I believed that if I had been brought face to face with him, I could not have uttered one reproach. I should have loved him so well still – though he fascinated me no longer – I should have held in so much tenderness the memory of my affection for him, that I think I should have been as weak as a spirit-wounded child, in all but the entertainment of a thought we could ever be re-united.' David goes on to apostrophize him directly: 'Yes, Steerforth, long removed from the scenes of this poor history! My sorrow may bear involuntary witness against you at the Judgment Throne; but my angry thoughts or my reproaches never will, I know!'[16] There is a mystery about Steerforth's 'inborn power of attraction' which is difficult to explain, for he is shown to be a snob (of course David is hardly in a position to condemn him for this), an egoist, a bully, and a cad. It has been argued by Angus Wilson[17] that Dickens's evident partiality has to do with the fact that Steerforth despises the world and puts other values above work. As for Dostoevsky, he certainly did not set much store by worldly achievement, and so this might have been a reason for him as well to share the special interest taken in Steerforth by his creator, but there is something more that must surely have drawn him: Steerforth's destructiveness and reckless squandering of his gifts. If Steerforth were forced to do something he might turn out to be a dilettante of a kind not unrelated to Henry Gowan ('all this was a brilliant game, played for the excitement of the moment, for the employment of high spirits, in the thoughtless love of superiority, in a mere wasteful careless course of winning what was worthless to him, and next minute thrown away . . .').[18] As it is, there is something compelling about the suggestion of his capacity for great achievement which he fails to realize. There is something compelling, too, about his freedom from ordinary laws. All this we find again in Stavrogin, who has in addition one gift which benefits others though not himself: the ability to connect ideas in powerful new schemes. Inasmuch as Stavrogin turns out to be no ordinary dilettante in his attempts to prove himself, he redeems the daemonic promise in Steerforth. In the end, however, all the wealth of possibility opened to him by his will-power and by his freedom from convention turns out to be illusory.

Perhaps an obscure sense of having overestimated Steerforth's capacity for greatness led Dostoevsky, in his next novel, to draw on one of his lesser actions[19] and exaggerate its meanness. When Steerforth first meets young David at Salem House, he takes him under his protection (which David very much needs), but at the same time takes charge of the money given to David by his mother and Peggotty, and forthwith spends it all on 'prog' for the boys in his bedroom (including David). In *A Raw Youth* Arkady's mother – a simple woman, towards whom Arkady is as patronizing as is David to Mr Peggotty and Ham – visits him at his school, and gives him four twenty-kopeck pieces wrapped in a handkerchief (instead of the paper used by David's mother). The money is promptly confiscated by Lambert, an out-and-out bully (and later a blackmailer), and spent on chocolate and pies, which the children of patrician families do not even have the grace to share with the unhappy Arkady.

Peter Verkhovensky and Barnaby Rudge

Given the basic situation in *The Devils*, the task of Peter Verkhovensky as the agent of revolution is relatively easy. It is little wonder Dostoevsky found him turning into a comic figure (see above, p. 107); the talents of a leader better versed in political and social theory would have been wasted, while in a role of this importance and length a narrow-minded fanatic would be tedious if he were treated seriously. The fact that Dostoevsky used an actual occurrence as the germ of his story has stood in the way of a proper understanding of this character. As Dostoevsky himself indicated, he was not interested in the historical circumstances, nor did he wish to produce a psychological study of Nechaev. At the same time, to present Peter Verkhovensky as essentially a caricature on the Russian radicals, as many critics have done, is to obscure the power of Dostoevsky's insight. It can be a useful corrective to see him as a conventional literary character deriving from Dickens, which is what I take him to be.

In a book where so many characters are haunted by ideas it is striking that the ideology of Peter Verkhovensky, the revolutionary leader, hardly seems to matter. All we are given is a description of his programme for action. Beliefs do not interest him except as they afford a means of manipulating the persons holding them. His attitude to society is of no greater importance than his politics, and his treatment of his father is of a piece with his attempts to sow discord. He is conceived entirely as a man of petty motive and feeling; we can readily accept the reason suggested for his dislike of Shatov – that Shatov once spat at him. In fact, he behaves very much as a stage villain. He appears to know everything and penetrate everywhere; walks into Madame Stavrogina's drawing-room seemingly possessed of information of vital importance at a key moment; claims to have seen Liputin pinching his wife in the privacy of his bedroom. He uses his voice to insinuate himself into people's minds, and when he calls on Stavrogin in his study, we are constantly aware of his tone and his manner (pt. II, ch. 1, iii): he 'whispers quickly and with an amazingly naïve air'; he 'waves his hands, scattering his words like peas'; 'reels off' [*zavertet'sia*]; 'rattles off' [*zatreshchat'sia*]; 'prattles' [*zataratorit'*]; and 'jumps up waving his hands, as if to ward off questions' when in fact no questions are being asked. He goes away, and Dostoevsky writes: 'Maybe he thought as he disappeared that on being left alone Nicholas Stavrogin would begin to hammer on the wall with his fists, and of course he would have been glad to observe him if it had been possible.' This brings him quite close to some of Dickens's villains, as in the episode in which Ralph Nickleby so provokes Newman Noggs that the clerk stands outside the office door, 'bestowing the most vigorous, scientific, and straight-forward blows upon the empty air'.[20] An entry in the notebooks suggests that Verkhovensky even had the psychology of a Dickensian villain:[21]

> Nechaev in himself is all the same an *accidental and individual* being. (Only he takes everyone to be like himself – and *in that he is mistaken* to the point of disgusting stupidity . . .
> . . . abstract cunning and complete ignorance of reality.
> Where he understands reality
> either he makes clever and almost brilliant use of it
> *or* through his one-sided understanding of the facts – he explains them and addresses them to the most stupid purposes.

Like Ralph Nickleby, Jonas Chuzzlewit, and Mr Pecksniff, he underestimates people through thinking that they have the same motivation as himself.

Can it be shown that Peter Verkhovensky derives from Dickens? His villain's psychology is not in itself very significant (even devils can be fooled). And it might be felt that any attempt to make him into a melodramatic villain leaves out of account a scene in which Verkhovensky acquires a certain depth – his impassioned appeal to Stavrogin in 'Ivan-the-Tsarevich':

> 'We shall proclaim destruction – because and because again this simple idea is so fascinating! . . . We shall set fires going – We shall set legends going. . . . And troubles will begin! Such a rocking there'll be as the world has never seen – Russia will be covered in fog, and the earth will weep for its old gods – So and then we will unloose – whom?'
> 'Whom?'
> 'Ivan-the-Tsarevich.'
> 'W-h-o-o-m?'
> 'Ivan-the-Tsarevich. You! You!'
> Stavrogin thought a minute. 'The pretender?' he suddenly asked, looking in profound amazement at the frenzied man. 'So this, at last, is your plan.'
> 'We shall say he is "hiding" ', Verkhovensky said quietly, in some kind of amorous whisper, as if he were really drunk. 'Do you know what this word, "hiding", means? But he will appear, he will appear. We will set going a better legend than any of the Old Believers [*skoptsy*]. . . . And the main thing is – a new force

will be moving. And that is what is needed, that's what they're crying for. After all, what is there in socialism? It has destroyed the old forces, without putting any new ones in. . . . Every peasant in every domain will know it's rumoured somewhere there is a hollow-oak where petitions are to be put. And the earth will moan its moan, "A new, righteous law is coming", and the sea will rise in turmoil, and the knockabout stage [*balagan*] will crash down, and then we shall think of setting up a structure of stone. For the first time! *We* shall do the building, we, we alone!' (pt. II, ch. 8, pp. 440ff.)

Here, of course, we are presented with Peter Verkhovensky's own particular myth, to which the forces of destruction are to be harnessed. But whereas Kirillov and Shatov have to struggle towards their myths and cannot quite grasp how effective they will be, Peter Verkhovensky's vision of destruction channelled and controlled by Ivan-the-Tsarevich seems almost to be sensuously present. We recognize that his vision is not so much something belonging to the man as it *is* the man. He is a personification of Unrest, Intrigue, and Revolution. His appeal to Stavrogin adds little to his complexity of thought and motive. Moreover, it is, I think, this speech that points to an influence from Dickens.

Critics in recent years have resurrected Dickens's first novel about rebellion, *Barnaby Rudge*. There, in a society characterized by twisted emotions and strained master-servant and father-son relationships, we find an Association being formed to mount an attack on Popery (and incidentally on Property). Its leader is Lord George Gordon, while the chief organizer is Gashford, who knows almost as well as Peter Verkhovensky the forces that can be unleashed under 'the mantle of religion'. There is a resurgence of primitive beliefs and legends; Gashford speaks of 'a crisis like the present, when Queen Elizabeth, the maiden monarch, weeps within her tomb, and Bloody Mary, with a brow of gloom and shadow stalks triumphant'. He inspires his leader by appealing to the thrill of power:

'They cried to be led on against the Papists, they vowed a dreadful vengeance on their heads, they roared like men possessed –'
  'But not by devils,' said his lord.
  'By devils! my lord. By angels.' . . .

'When you warmed,' said the secretary, looking sharply at the other's downcast eyes, which brightened slowly as he spoke; 'when you warmed into that noble outbreak; when you told them that you were never of the lukewarm or the timid tribe, and bade them take heed that they were prepared to follow one who would lead them on, though to the very death . . . when they cried "No Popery!" and you cried "No; not even if we wade in blood," and they threw up their hats and cried "Hurrah! not even if we wade in blood; No Popery! Lord George! Down with the Papists – Vengeance on their heads:" when this was said and done, and a word from you, my lord, could raise or still the tumult – ah! then I felt what greatness was indeed, and thought, When was there ever a power like this of Lord George Gordon's.'

And Gordon responds, as Stavrogin does not, to this release of elemental forces and passions: 'They may cough and jeer, and groan in Parliament, and call me fool and madman, but which of them can raise this human sea and make it swell and roar at pleasure?' John Grueby, Lord George Gordon's faithful retainer, understands better than his master what all this is leading to: 'One of these evenings, when the weather gets warmer and Protestants are thirsty, they'll be pulling London down.'[22]

Gashford and Verkhovensky are cast in similar roles, and adopt a similar strategy. As Dickens says (ch. 37): 'To surround anything, however monstrous or ridiculous, with an air of mystery, is to invest it with a secret charm, and power of attraction which to the crowd is irresistible. False priests, false prophets, false doctors, false patriots, false prodigies of every kind, veiling their proceedings in mystery, have always addressed themselves at an immense advantage to the popular credulity.' Strange pamphlets appear (this of course is part of the work of any agitator); rumours about the size of the Protestant Association and of Peter Verkhovensky's network of cells help to bring new adherents. But a charismatic leader is needed. We note that Stavrogin is, like Lord George Gordon, an aristocrat. Verkhovensky says to him: 'An aristocrat coming over to democracy is fascinating'; and wants to make him the God of Sabaoth. Gordon has the triple sanction of rank, religion, and popular election:[23]

'. . . I will be worthy of the motto on my coat of arms, "Called and chosen and faithful." '

'Called', said the secretary, 'by Heaven.'
'I am.'
'Chosen by the people.'
'Yes.'
'Faithful to both.'
'To the block!'

Of course, Stavrogin will not accept the role of leader, whereas of Gordon we are told: 'This lord was sincere in his violence and in his wavering. A nature prone to false enthusiasm, and the vanity of being leader, were the worst qualities apparent in his composition.' Indeed, Gordon is so given to new fancies that, at the height of his power as president of the Great Protestant Association, he dreams he is a Jew, and later he becomes a convert. Stavrogin explores old religions and new (his travels to Egypt and Jerusalem could be connected with his quest), but he lacks 'enthusiasm'. An entry in the notebooks says: 'The prince understands that enthusiasm could save him (for instance, monastic life, self-sacrifice through confession). But he is too lacking in moral feeling to have enthusiasm (partly because of unbelief).'[24]

In the scene in which Gashford fires his leader's imagination (ch. 35), he is busy 'taking the lion's share of the mulled wine'; and voracity is one of Verkhovensky's chief characteristics. Next time Gashford goes into Gordon's room at the Maypole, he is shown adjusting his 'countenance' and his manner in a very stagey way. 'With a smiling face, but still with looks of proud deference and humility', he approached the room, 'smoothing his hair down as he went, and humming a psalm tune.' Once inside, he 'took out a pen, and before dipping it in the inkstand, sucked it – to compose the fashion of his mouth perhaps, on which a smile was hovering yet.' Likewise Peter Verkhovensky, on emerging from Kirillov's room after a somewhat unsatisfactory conversation, tries 'to transform his displeased expression into a kind physiognomy'. As he and Stavrogin arrive shortly afterwards at the revolutionaries' meeting, he says, 'Compose your physiognomy, Stavrogin. I always compose mine when I go in. A bit more sombre, and that's all. Nothing more is needed. A very simple trick.'[25] Gashford exerts the same sort of control over the riots as Verkhovensky over the fête and the other events. 'Gashford walked stealthily about, listening to all he heard and diffusing or confirming whenever he had an opportunity, such false intelligence as suited his own purpose.' He attempts to make the rioters instruments of his own will. When Hugh steps out from the crowd and walks behind him along the pavement to find out whether he is pleased, Gashford replies, 'pinching his arm with such malevolence that his nails seemed to meet in the skin; "I would have you put some meaning into your work. Fools! Can you make no better bonfires than out of rags and scraps? Can you burn nothing whole?" ' In *The Devils,* when the revolutionaries gather on the morning after the fête, Shigalev challenges Verkhovensky to explain the reason for his displeasure when his own programme of arson, stirring up scandal and popular discontent, and undermining local government, is being carried out. Verkhovensky accuses them of having too much independence of will.[26] His motive is, like Gashford's, partly an impatient wish for mass destruction and partly spite. Gashford wishes to revenge himself on Mr Haredale (after being knocked down by him); Verkhovensky has a long-standing grudge against Shatov, whom he wants the revolutionaries to murder. Both men could as easily be spies as revolutionaries.

For the rest it is necessary to turn to another character who, with Gashford, forms the 'essence of the great Association' – Sir John Chester (for Dickens the greatest villain of all). An unscrupulous defender of wealth, privilege, and social appearances, he bears direct responsibility for the riots in a threefold capacity: he is a member of the Parliament whose bad laws are responsible for the existence of the London mob; he is the father of Hugh, a bastard and an outcast, who becomes a mob leader; he manipulates both Gashford and Hugh, and through them stirs up agitation against Catholics for political and private purposes of his own. He too is animated by spite against Haredale, and together he and Gashford 'plot in secrecy and safety, and leave exposed posts to the duller wits'. His chief weapons are intrigue, blackmail, and some simple psychological tricks.

Verkhovensky's relationship with Gashford chiefly concerns their function in their respective plots, whereas his relationship with Chester is mostly a matter of the methods the men use. Chester establishes a complete hold over Hugh by threatening to turn him in 'for robbery on the king's highway' (an offence for which he could hang). Chester is then able to infiltrate Hugh into Gordon's movement, and so to reduce the danger of compromising himself. Consider this exchange when Hugh returns after going to enlist and Chester asks him what he has been up to:

'No harm at all, master,' growled Hugh, with humility. 'I have only done as you ordered.'

'As I *what?*' returned Sir John.

'Well then,' said Hugh uneasily, 'as you advised, or said I ought, or said I might, or said that you would do, if you was me. Don't be so hard upon me master.' (ch. 40, p. 303)

Verkhovensky is more concerned to compromise others than to avoid being compromised himself, and his attempts are numerous and varied. He persuades Madame Von Lembke to make all sorts of ill-considered plans for the fête, tries to bind his five-man cell through an act of bloodshed, and wants to implicate Stavrogin in the murder of the Lebiadkins. In the last of these aims, he hardly succeeds, but an exchange between him and Liputin after Captain Lebiadkin has been found murdered is oddly reminiscent of Chester and Hugh:

'You were ordered to send Lebiadkin off and you were given money for that purpose, and what did you do? If you had sent him off nothing would have happened.'

'But didn't you yourself have the idea that it would be a good thing to let him read some of his poems?'

'An idea is not an order. The order was to send him off.'

'An order. Rather a strong word – On the contrary, you specifically ordered me to hold up his departure.'

'You are wrong and have shown stupidity and self-will.'

(pt. III, ch. 4, i, pp. 567f.)

Verkhovensky is, of course, a blunderer (as he himself admits, he is a mediocrity – this is part of the secret of his success and part of his significance in the novel). So 'consummate' is Chester's art that he manages to establish total ascendancy over Hugh, an unusually free being. 'Hugh's submission was complete. He dreaded him beyond description; and felt that accident and artifice had spun a web about him, which at a touch from such a master hand as his, would bind him to the gallows.' With rather greater reason, though with less skill, Verkhovensky acquires almost as powerful a hold over his agents: 'They felt that suddenly they had been trapped like flies in the web of an enormous spider; they fumed, but trembled with fear.'[27]

One of Chester's devices in dealing with people is to put them at a disadvantage. In the course of his meetings with Hugh, or his legitimate son Edward, or Mr Haredale, we see him attending to his breakfast or to his dessert, sipping his wine, and paring his nails, as though the conversation was incidental to the satisfaction of his physical needs. Dostoevsky uses the same tricks for Verkhovensky (and uses them too for Prince Valkovsky in *The Insulted and Injured*). Whereas in Chester they are signs of perfect social complacency, in Verkhovensky they express the crude, undisguised appetites of the man. During the gathering at Virginsky's house Verkhovensky interrupts the proceedings to demand a glass of cognac. Then when Shigalev is expounding his social theories (in which he deduces absolute despotism from a postulate of absolute freedom), Verkhovensky calls for a pair of scissors, and starts to cut his nails (to the admiration of the female student from St Petersburg, who sees in this a model of emancipated behaviour). At the same time, his power over his followers is far from complete. When he and Liputin are on their way to Kirillov to arrange the time of his suicide, Verkhovensky insists on stopping so that he can treat himself to a steak. The richly comic description of Liputin's jealous and repelled reaction as he watches him devouring it, suggests Verkhovensky is dangerously unaware of the men he manipulates.[28]

Discretion is necessary in the use of literary parallels. The programme of the actual Nechaev was laid down in the 'Catechism of a Revolutionary', a document which Nechaev brought with him to Russia, and which is now thought to be in greater or lesser part the work of Bakunin. Apart from a fascinating statement of the qualities required of a revolutionary (and these hardly seem to characterize Peter Verkhovensky), the 'Catechism' set out the tasks that needed to be performed: a revolutionary had to penetrate everywhere; get hold of the secrets of highly placed persons for purposes of blackmail; encourage the authorities to carry out tough repressive policies (so that the people would revolt); compromise men of liberal principles and force them to collaborate; and form an alliance with the 'wild world of brigands, the only true revolutionaries in Russia'. There were a number of other tasks, all designed to bring about 'fearful, total, universal and remorseless destruction'. There are obvious parallels between the 'Catechism' and the novel: Verkhovensky's attempts to discredit the governor and his wife; the use he makes of the liberal thinkers in Stephan Trofimovich's circle; his relations with the escaped convict Fedka; the acts of terrorism. Yet the parallels are almost certainly not the result of a direct influence, and the 'Catechism' is unlikely to have been of any material importance to Dostoevsky; it was not published until July 1871,[29] and an entry in the notebooks dated 13 May of that year states: 'The association can act through violence, lies, deception, murder, slander, and robbery, so long as it has not won the upper hand but is still fighting. For that matter, it can continue to act in that way.'[30] It would be silly to infer that Dostoevsky must have had access to the 'Catechism' in the early stages of composition, as if he had no other opportunities of finding out about revolutionary aims and methods. Of course, it would be equally shortsighted to claim that Dostoevsky used blackmail and intrigue because he found them used by Sir John Chester. But the parallels are sufficiently telling that it can be plausibly suggested that the way in which he uses them does derive from this character.

To identify literary sources for Peter Verkhovensky is not to deny that he could also have historical sources. But the notion of historical sources gives rise to certain difficulties here. We already know that Peter Verkhovensky was not a study of the historical Nechaev. What about the personal experience Dostoevsky could have drawn upon? His 'revolutionary' activity was not confined to attending the Petrashevsky circle beginning in 1847.[31] Several of the participants, weary of discussions about the future organization of life under Fourier's system and like matters, decided to hold some private sessions on their own. This group, which is known as the Durov circle, included Dostoevsky, and the man they looked to as leader was Speshnev. Beyond the fact that the group managed to get hold of a printing press and to distribute propaganda, there is little first-hand evidence about their activities, but from what is known of the opinions of the different men, as put forward in the public discussions and elsewhere, it is possible that they thought of attempting to free the serfs through insurrection. At some of the meetings of the Petrashevsky circle the operation and organization of a secret society were considered (the topic was introduced by some members of the Durov group), and it was decided that one way of safeguarding secrecy would be to institute the death penalty for treachery. A draft of a declaration to be signed by members of a revolutionary group was found among Speshnev's papers; in it a member bound himself to fight in every possible way when the central committee decided the time for an uprising had come, and undertook to procure new members and to get them to sign the same pledge, which was to be sent to the committee. But whether the Durov circle was established on these principles is a matter of pure speculation. There is a hint or two that Dostoevsky thought of establishing relations with the Old Believers; and it is known that this was a question discussed by the radical members of the Petrashevsky circle. And he was very much aware of the power and fascination of Speshnev, who is often considered to be an influence on Stavrogin. But the scanty biographical information provides no good parallel to the basic desire of Verkhovensky and Gashford – to spread revolution and achieve power with the help of a princely leader acting in the name of primitive religion and super-stition. The available facts might be made to fit into such a scheme, but since the scheme derives from *The Devils*, the facts will hardly serve to 'explain' the novel. On the other hand, a very similar scheme can be pointed to in *Barnaby Rudge*. Objections of the same kind apply to other historical sources which have been suggested, and in particular to Grossman's claim that Bakunin was the prototype of Stavrogin. The historical facts have to be constructed out of the novel, or alterna-tively they are not unique and fit a number of other historical figures. We do not know which materials from life and history Dostoevsky was using – nor in what way. We can point to the ready-made parallels in *Barnaby Rudge*, and although we have no direct evidence that Dostoevsky had read this novel (see above, p. 48), none of the other sources suggested for Peter Verkhovensky provides such good evidence of an influence.

If literary evidence is to be believed, there are good grounds for Verkhovensky to call himself a 'scoundrel' – he is a villain whose fore-bears include Gashford and Chester. This could help to explain Stavrogin's emergence as the principal hero of the novel; if Dost-oevsky was working under Gashford's influence when he was devising Verkhovensky's role in the novel, he would have felt the need for a leader through whom Verkhovensky could work. To create a memor-able villain is not within every writer's reach. In a review published in *Grazhdanin* in 1873, and which is attributed to Dostoevsky,[32] two nihilists in Leskov's *Cathedral Folk* are attacked:

Not only are they not types, they are not even caricatures, because they are too completely lacking in the salt necessary for caricature. No, they are simply the creations of some nightmare. We regret that the poet ignored here the principle that negative types exist only in virtue of their poetic truth; thus if a negative type has the chief role in a work, he must astonish us with his force and energy of life ('The Miserly Knight', 'Richard III', etc.), so that we are seized with the thought 'God, what a wealth of life and what has it all gone to!' Or if the negative type, or rather figure, plays a secondary role, it must, at the very least, provide at any rate an additional colour – or else it is nothing, that is to say a complete failure on the part of the author.

Peter Verkhovensky is charged with a very Dickensian energy of life. His weakness is that he suffers from over-exposure. We can accept his ability to penetrate everywhere and to manipulate others, but begin to doubt it when we see too much of him; Dostoevsky should have trusted more to the magnetic power of this figure. If historical or psychological understanding is important, Peter Verkhovensky on his own cannot teach us very much. He is a conventional villain. The real danger lies in the social forces that give an evil or comic monstrosity a role. Verkhovensky belongs with the rabble which Dostoevsky makes little effort to understand:

> In troubled times of uncertainty or transition, scum of various kinds always and everywhere appear. I am not referring to the so-called 'progressives', who always hasten before anyone else (this being their chief concern), and have a more or less definite aim, even if a very stupid one. No, I am referring only to the rabble. In every transitional time, the rabble, which are to be found in any society, are raised, and are not only without aim, but have not even the trace of a thought, merely expressing with all their strength unrest and impatience. (pt. III, ch. 1, i, p. 481)

The real source of disintegration so clearly lies within society itself that our curiosity about the rabble is hardly aroused as it is about Dickens's mob (perhaps Dickens's failure to account for his mob seems a weakness partly because it had an actual historical existence, and might be imagined to have had some definite purposes of its own). Peter Verkhovensky, the progressives, the rabble – all are the agents of disease which take over a weakened organism. The horror and evil which erupt on the night of the fête – drunkenness, debauchery, fire, murder, the wild dancing of the 'Kamarinskaia', and the collapse of order and authority – are everything Peter Verkhovensky stands for. And out of this chaos Dostoevsky creates a sense of those things that have mattered and always will matter for society.

Stepan Trofimovich Verkhovensky

Dostoevsky's distinctive strength is that he can share in the general corruption and yet create a sense of loss (Dickens, as is well known, fluctuates between condemnation of the rebels and secret identification with them). It is very much a time of transition ('from what and to what . . . I do not know, and I do not think anybody knows').[33] Dostoevsky's tone as a narrator is of the same gossipy kind we can find in his Liputins and Liamshins. He feels the pull of disintegration, and is very much aware of the pull.

> A big fire at night always produces an impression both teasing and cheering. This is the principle behind fireworks, but with them fire forms elegant and regular configurations, and in view of their complete harmlessness, they produce a light and playful impression, such as after a glass of champagne. A real conflagration is something quite different: the horror and at the same time a sort of feeling of personal danger, along with the cheering impression of fire by night, produce in the spectator (not, of course, the one whose own house is burning) a certain shaking up of the brain, and a kind of appeal to his own destructive instincts, such as, alas! lurk in every soul, even in the mildest and most family-minded of titular councillors. . . .
> To be sure the same amateur of night fire will throw himself into the flames to save a burning child or an old woman, but that is quite another matter. (pt. III, ch. 2, p. 537)

Because of this self-awareness, Dostoevsky can organize his themes effectively and create a sense of beauty and value. Stepan Trofimovich's death reminds us (as did the scenes with Shatov and his wife) that the meaning of a man's life lies in something more than bare appetency.

Stepan Trofimovich represents a generation dominated not only by Belinsky, Chaadaev, Herzen, and Granovsky but also by Hegel and, as we find mentioned in the opening paragraphs of the book, by George Sand and Dickens. And it is possible to recognize a very Dickensian figure underneath the Idealist of the Forties.

Like General Ivolgin he is a variation on the Micawber-and-Dorrit-type of character. He has cast himself in a role to which he fails to live up. He sees himself as a man courted and admired for his intellect; believes that he has spent his life working for progress; imagines that he is persecuted by the police. But, as is made abundantly clear, all this rests on a delusion. Right from the start he is seen as an actor. In a characteristic Dostoevskian procedure, the narrator writes: 'Not that I would compare him to an actor in the theatre – Heaven forbid, especially as I honour him.' Not surprisingly, the slur sticks. He is really a child, and in need of a nurse. He does not pay his debts. He is constantly breaking down and crying at his own degradation. He finds himself defeated by the 'whirl of convergent circumstances'. The parallels with Micawber and Dorrit are obvious, and at the same time sufficiently general that a close comparison of the kind conducted for Ivolgin would not be profitable. For all his folly and blindness, and for all the narrator's exasperation with him, Stepan Trofimovich emerges as one of Dostoevsky's most lovable characters. As we see him at the opening of the novel, he and his friends are living under a spell. There is a sense of arrested time. His talk is dominated by the ideas of twenty or thirty years before; his relations with his patroness are locked in an unhealthy pattern. Yet in the course of the novel it turns out that this frozen situation, from which he is so rudely awakened, contains the seeds of his salvation. Stepan Trofimovich has been most truly himself in his relations with Madame Stavrogina, in something of the way of Mr Dorrit in his relations with his daughter in the Marshalsea. And as Mr Micawber remains true to his hope of something turning up, so Stepan Trofimovich remains true to the 'Great Idea'.

Stepan Trofimovich embodies the false hopes of his generation. Belief in perfectible man, brotherhood, and the fundamental importance of enlightenment was dangerous because it was divorced from a sense of national tradition. What saves him is in part his laziness, his weakness, his inconsistency – his humanity. He has despised the popular religion as a superstition, without ever making his dislike a basis for action. After each failure he has fallen back on his patroness for consolation. In the revolutionary turmoil his ideals and his belief in the virtues of the heart are derided, and even Madame Stavrogina turns against him. For the first time, he discovers that this is the one relationship that has mattered to him, and that the ideals he and she believed in, but never did anything about, were all that made life worth living. He runs away to die among the Russian people he has always claimed to love. While he can hardly be said to discover them (the glimpses we have of the peasants are at best ambiguous, if not ominous), we can see him as a Don Quixote defending his vision of beauty. His ideals might be hopelessly unadapted to and subversive of Russian reality; none the less they were noble and universal ideals, and could lead him to salvation. His death redeems the generation that first introduced Dickens to Russia.

Notes

1 A. G. Dostoevskaia, *Vospominaniia* (Moscow-Leningrad, 1925), p. 130.
2 No. 345, *Pis'ma*, vol. 2 (see, too, letters nos. 318 and 346).
3 *Zapisnye tetrady F. M. Dostoevskogo*, ed. E. N. Konshina (Moscow-Leningrad, 1935).
4 See A. L. Bem, 'Evoliutsiia obraza Stavrogina', a typescript deposited in the British Museum [1931-9].
5 'Steerforth and Stavrogin', *Slavonic and East European Review*, 27 (1949), 469–88.
6 *Diary of a Writer* (1873). *Dnevnik pisatelia* (Paris, 1951), vol. 1, p. 351.
7 *The Devils*, pt. II, ch. 10, i, pp. 464f. (in *Sobranie sochinenii*, vol. 7).
8 Pt. II, ch. 1, iii, p. 240; ch. 1, vii, pp. 265ff.
9 Pt. II, ch. 4, i, pp. 313f.
10 Pt II, ch. 1, vii, p. 270. A closer approximation to *muchitel'stvo* than 'torture' would be 'torturedom'.
11 Pt. II, ch. 1, v; pt. III, ch. 6, ii.
12 Only with Kirillov does Stavrogin have an equal relationship; Kirillov does not need him to act a role, although ironically Stavrogin accomplishes what Kirillov has failed to do.
13 *Diary of a Writer* (1877), January, ch. 2, iv. *Dnevnik pisatelia*, vol. 3, p. 42.
14 *Zapis'nye tetradi*, p. 179.
15 *Copperfield*, ch. 20, p. 297; ch. 29, pp. 433, 436f.; ch. 55, p. 795.
16 *Copperfield*, ch. 32, p. 455.
17 'The Heroes and Heroines of Dickens', *Dickens and the Twentieth Century*, ed. Gross and Pearson (London, 1962).
18 *Copperfield*, ch. 21, p. 311.
19 See Futrell, 'Dostoyevsky and Dickens', *English Miscellany*, ed. Praz, 7 (1956), 81ff.
20 *Nickleby*, ch. 28.
21 *Zapisnye tetradi*, p. 276.
22 *Barnaby*, ch. 35, pp. 264, 268ff.; ch. 45, p. 339.
23 *Barnaby*, ch. 35, p. 270; *The Devils*, pt. II, ch. 8, pp. 438, 441.
24 *Zapisnye tetradi*, p. 284.
25 *Barnaby*, ch. 36, pp. 272f.; *The Devils*, pt. II, ch. 6, vi, p. 396 and ch. 6, vii, p. 406. In the translation of *Barnaby* in *Otechestvennye zapiski* in 1842 –

a very accurate one – 'countenance' is translated as *fizinomiaa*, but 'to compose' becomes 'to straighten'.

26 *The Devils*, pt. III, ch. 4, i, pp. 570f.; *Barnaby*, ch. 50, p. 385; ch. 52, p. 401. Other possible parallels: the scenes in which Verkhovensky walks along the pavement, chasing after Stavrogin, or pursued by Liputin.

27 *Barnaby*, ch. 23, p. 179; *The Devils*, pt. III, ch. 4, ii, p. 574.

28 *Barnaby*, ch. 12, p. 92; ch. 15, p. 118; ch. 32, pp. 243ff.; *The Devils*, pt. II, ch. 7, ii, pp. 419ff.; pt. III, ch. 4, ii, p. 576.

29 By which time *The Devils*, pt. II, ch. 2, had been published and the main design of the novel was apparent. See Grossman and Polonsky, *Spor o Bakunine i Dostoevskom* (Leningrad, 1926).

30 *Zapisnye tetradi*, p. 279.

31 See A. S. Dolinin, 'Dostoevsky sredi petrashevtsev', *Zven'ia*, ed. V. Bonch-Burevich, 6 (1936), 512–45.

32 See V. V. Vinogradov, *Problema avtorstva i teoriia stilei* (Moscow, 1961), pp. 506–14, and 516.

33 Pt. III, ch. 1, i, p. 481.

7

The Brothers Karamazov

Dostoevsky's last novel forces us, as no other of his works, to consider questions about the truth or falsehood of ideology. It has its Dickensian qualities – we might start with the rings on the investigating lawyer's fingers (a touch of Wemmick?) or with Grushenka's Polish friends (Job Trotter and Jingle?) – but if *The Brothers Karamazov* (1879–80) has a place in this book surely it is in relation to the view we have taken of Dostoevsky as a social novelist. The notion that without God there is no morality served as a structuring principle in *The Idiot* and *The Devils*, where the Russian God was dying and society disintegrating. The Russian dilemma went back to the forceful Westernization of the country by Peter the Great; there were, on the one hand, the old and increasingly meaningless authorities of the State and the Church; on the other – the new social and economic realities, and a fertile ground of discontent among the aristocrats, landowners, and priests' sons raised on Western ideas. In exploring this dilemma Dostoevsky found that Christ's story had lost its power – the paradox within it was now felt by men to be a contradiction rather than a miracle or mystery – and further that without a myth Russia could not for long survive. But the myths congenial to his contemporaries' imaginations were demoniac ones; they might serve for a revolution, not for a rebirth of national consciousness.

In *The Brothers Karamazov* Dostoevsky does not simply assume that there is no morality without God. He tests this proposition, approaching it by way of questions as to whether man can still accept Christian theology, whether a morality not rooted in metaphysics can exist, whether a Christian morality still has something to offer, and whether a man can sanction murder (even if he cannot bring himself to commit it). *The Brothers Karamazov* is Dostoevsky's most philosophical novel, but the questions were not abstract; they were of immediate importance for his Russian contemporaries. If the disappearance of God left the individual in a logically or psychologically intolerable position, and if the dying God turned out to have some forgotten or unsuspected qualities, then the national consciousness might yet be re-created. And since the Russian crisis was, as Dostoevsky saw it, a result of the importation of the materialistic, European civilization, it was possible that any solution he found might contain an answer to such problems of bourgeois man as the fragmentation of society (epitomized in the feeling that your fellow man stinks) and the 'tyranny of things and habits' which comes about when freedom means the 'multiplication and rapid satisfaction of needs'.[1]

The particular situation of Russia enters into the novel. The prosecutor proclaims in his speech at the trial that the country is in a critical pass, and identifies each of the brothers with one aspect of the crisis. The lawyer's plea that Dimitry should be acquitted even if he were guilty, for a man would be justified in killing a father such as old Fedor, recalls the acquittal of Vera Zasulich after her public assassination of the Governor-General of St Petersburg in 1878. Alongside the extremist views of the alienated minority subsists the primitive imagination of the people, for whom the land is still the battleground of devils and gods. Father Ferapont appears in the cell where Zosima's corpse lies stinking in order to assert the power of his god (bk. VIII, ch. 1): 'He turned toward the setting sun, raised both arms and – as if he were mowed down – fell with a great scream: "My Lord has vanquished! Christ has vanquished the setting sun!" ' Of course Dostoevsky himself is no primitive; he establishes truth not by appealing to some particular god, but to human understanding and experience. And here he brings his fullest view of human nature to bear on the questions he debates. His concern is not so much what was happening to his society as to look again for a basis for community, even though charity, compassion, and childlike laughter had proved inadequate. Whether his view of man and his quest are in some way affected by his own position as a member of the alienated intelligentsia is a question to bear in mind.

The nature of the Russian problem is underlined by the discussion of miracles running through the novel. What can bring about a miracle, and what are the signs of one? A miracle depends on the faith of many, and it is the unexpected. It would be too obvious and vulgar a miracle if Zosima's body did not decompose; too many people expect it. And their belief is of the wrong kind; a miracle is a result of faith rather than an object of faith. The true miracle now would lie in bringing about a new state of feeling, a feeling of union with man and the world, the kind of feeling from which other 'miracles' can flow. It is the happiness Alesha is able to find when Grushenka shares his grief at Zosima's death and over the scandal round his rotting body; what she has done, she says, is no more than the mean old woman whose one charitable deed in all her life was to give away a little onion; yet a 'little onion' is enough for Alesha to be reborn as he kneels beside Father Zosima's coffin and listens to the words about the miracle at Cana of Galilee. In the words of Father Zosima (bk. VI, ch. 2, d): 'It is a spiritual, psychological matter. If the world is to be made anew, people must turn on to another road in their psyche.'

There are many attempts to find what the nature of the universe is and what the pattern of men's lives should therefore be. Father Ferapont represents the ultimate corruption of the attempt to behold the fowls of the air and to consider the lilies of the field, and to take no thought for life. Fasting and prayer have freed him from the chains of earthly bread; he can live off nature's superfluity of wild berries and mushrooms. Yet it seems he can assert the beneficence of a harsh world only by cutting himself off from other men and hating them. Narrow legalism, vindictiveness, and superstition characterize this medieval figure. All the others accept the need for earthly bread and thus for society. Zosima's sense of the oneness of things is the expression of a man who has the passionate make-up of a Dimitry and it is asserted in the face of the rationalist objections that can be made by an Ivan. In nature we see God (bk. VI, ch. 2,b): 'Every blade of grass, every beetle, ant, and golden bee, all quite amazingly know their way, without having a mind, they bear witness to God's mystery, they continually accomplish it themselves.' Once you know this, you know that the kingdom of heaven can exist on earth: 'we alone are Godless and stupid, and do not understand that life is paradise, for we need only want to understand that, and it will at once come about in all its glory, and we shall embrace each other and weep.' The difficulty lies in making men *want* to understand. The place where this vision or feeling of the universe is harboured is the monastery. The problem is to carry it outside, or alternatively to create some equivalent of the monastic life outside the walls within which it had been confined.[2] And this depends on whether men are held back simply by prosaic common sense, as Ivan's Devil suggests, and whether ethics can recapture its traditional concern with every aspect of behaviour.

One possibility is for the Church to become all-embracing, so that no one could conceive what to exist outside it would be. Ivan had argued in the article which brought him to the attention of the public, that the Church was by its nature antithetical to the State; the two could never compromise. The Church was bound to take over and absorb the State. When everybody saw himself as part of the Church, criminals could hardly exist. A man would be unable to cut himself off from everything that gave life meaning; in so far as he did and punishment was necessary, he would be regenerated rather than alienated. Of course, the impossibility of this ever coming about is the reason why Ivan's article is received with interest by atheists; the innermost idea of the Church could never be realized. Ivan himself is under no illusions. He says in the 'Legend of the Grand Inquisitor' that man wants earthly bread and authority, and at the same time is a rebel. Hence, in the end, if society is to be unified, it will be through the Church being transformed into a State, and not through the State being absorbed into the Church.

The authoritarian solution is not, of course, one that Dostoevsky wishes to adopt – certainly not in the Grand Inquisitor's form. He is concerned with the ways open to individuals, and the help an existing institution, Russian Orthodoxy, could give them. His appeal is to men's conscience and feelings, as in Dimitry's vision of the suffering babe (bk. IX, ch. 8), which leads to his wish to share the unhappiness and hard work of the convicts (bk. XI, ch. 4). To go through with this wish entails being treated like a murderer by the prison guards, which is more than Dimitry can take. If he runs away he proposes to set up as a farmer, together with Grushenka, somewhere in a remote part of Russia. What his life there would amount to Dostoevsky does not say. We are led to ask how and where in Dostoevsky's world meaningful work is to be found. All we are given is what Dostoevsky shows us of the practical activity of Alesha Karamazov (we must bear in mind, for what it is worth, that Dostoevsky regarded *The Brothers Karamazov* as only the first part of a larger work). From the start Alesha has the clearer vision which comes to Dimitry too late. He listens to people without judging or, at any rate, condemning them. Like Zosima he tries to help people who want to be helped, and does so by looking for something within a man's own consciousness which can help him to accept his own self and the world. Alesha's philanthropy is based on the assumption of the beauty and harmony of the world, although this beauty and harmony is not something he experiences until he returns from Grushenka to pray beside Zosima's coffin. And yet doubts must persist as to what Alesha can actually do.

Dostoevsky would like to establish morality on a basis of states of mind, and one of the valuable things he does in this novel is to explore the difficulties which arise if your concern is with intentions and feelings rather than with actions. The stress on purity of heart and sins of intention is of course one of the important legacies of Christianity. To the extent that the Karamazov brothers have similar feelings, they are similarly guilty. Ivan and Dimitry have both desired their father's death. Ivan is restrained by habits and upbringing, but almost unconsciously connives with Smerdiakov to have old Fedor murdered; afterwards he is paralysed with feelings of guilt. Dimitry would like to accept his punishment because he too has wanted to kill.

If one believes that the important thing in morality is what a man feels and not what he does, and if one accepts that harmony characterizes the universe, one may be particularly inclined to accept that whatever happens is a sign of the basic oneness of the universe. It is this recognition which is embodied in the recurrent statement that each is responsible – or rather guilty [*vinovat*] – for all. Zosima says (bk. VI, ch. 3,g): 'Everything is like an ocean, everything flows and is interconnected.' This oceanic feeling shapes the whole novel, and is reflected in a multitude of details. For instance, Grigory regards his six-fingered child as a dragon, and after the child's death adopts Smerdiakov, who turns into a real monster. More significantly: not only is each of the brothers involved in the killing of Fedor (Alesha mainly through his failure to look after Dimitry, for whom he is responsible) – but Alesha rebels against his spiritual father, Zosima, while Dimitry knocks down Grigory, who once acted as a father to him. The difficulty with an oceanic feeling of oneness and an ethic of being rather than of doing, is that, however closely they may agree with our sense of things, they leave us with little guidance how to conduct our affairs in a world where the stress is on achievement, change, and acquisition. The solution may lie in withdrawal or abdication. And for all of Dostoevsky's attempt to show that the practical man must be a believer and that Alesha's love is an active one, Dostoevsky's ultimate ideal seems to be largely contemplative. About the institution of Elders, he says (bk. I, ch. 5) that the existence of a holy man consoles a peasant for the world's injustice and sin. And perhaps the shadow of a holy man is enough – Zosima and Smerdiakov suggest that maybe the whole Church rests on seven righteous men or on one or two hermits saving themselves somewhere in the Egyptian desert.[3] The failure of the ethic of feeling is nowhere so vividly brought out as in Alesha's speech beside Iliusha's grave. He suggests that he and the boys will always be better people because they have been kind to Iliusha in his last illness and because they have buried him. Allowing for the greater circumstantial and psychological realism, and for the greater modesty and smaller rhetoric of Alesha's claims, the speech is as inadequate in its way as Dickens's performance after the death of Little Nell. It fails to deal with all the issues that have come before it in the novel, and does not convince us that the change in the children's state of feeling will be an important one.

If Dostoevsky sensed the inadequacy of Alesha's outlook, the realization was only a partial one. Otherwise he could not have treated so cursorily the humanist morality sketched by Ivan (in 'The Geological Catechism')[4] nor suggested that the goal of a humanist morality led in the short run to the principle that everything is allowed. His weakness as a philosopher is apparent here. But it is tempting to see what Dostoevsky makes of Dimitry in the light of some such realization. For another mode of salvation besides compassion is offered by this character – sexual love. Dimitry, to whom surely we respond more readily than to his brothers, is a measure of Dostoevsky's genius (he represents a striking departure in an artist approaching sixty). The poetry he quotes so readily, his readiness to embrace all contradictions, the passion breathing through his voice, the talk about golden-haired Phoebus, his sensuous description of the world – all are evidence of his great energy and love of life. Much of the interest he compels is independent of the issues of Orthodoxy versus atheism debated by Alesha and Ivan. In part the disjointedness which results is justified by the nature of Dostoevsky's undertaking; he was exploring the ways men had of overcoming alienation, and the distinctive sorts of interest we bring to bear on the individual characters are a tribute to Dostoevsky's success in conveying different modes of apprehending the world – in the case of the three brothers – physical, rational, and spiritual.[5]

There is a new breadth and relaxation in Dostoevsky's art in this novel; his central characters are less extreme types than in his previous work. There is also a relaxation of a more unsatisfactory sort. Dostoevsky does not test his characters and ideas as fully as he had done before. The disjointedness of Dostoevsky's art here is influenced by the peculiar situation he was describing. His previous novels had shown that the frame of society was disintegrating. Dostoevsky was clinging to what was left of it. Hence, it follows for Alesha that to love life is to love the Christian God and immortality. Because there was a lack of institutions and traditions to build on, Dostoevsky was forced to turn to the individual and to the Church in the hope of finding something to set against disintegration and revolution. His inconclusive attitude towards his solutions is in part justified because the situation he was exploring was still an open one. But if his commitment to the survival of his country was an asset in late nineteenth-century Russia, it now appears as a limitation. A common bond of feeling was unlikely to be found latent in a society which had become an assemblage of individuals. And by the time the Church was seen as an institution rather than as the expression of the spiritual life of the people, it was unlikely to play an important role either in awakening a conscience in men or in re-forming society.[6]

Dostoevsky's vision is affected in other ways too. We may or may not accept his claim that the alternative to man's enslavement in modern society lies in freedom from the tyranny of bodily needs (bk. VI, ch. 3,e). Yet for all the talk about freedom here and in the 'Legend of the Grand Inquisitor', Dostoevsky's solution is in fact authoritarian: it rests on obedience to an Elder, and it seems no coincidence that Dostoevsky lived in an authoritarian society which he defended (although he does uphold the freedom which we still regard as the most important one – of conscience). Then, too, his sense that we are each responsible for all is conveyed with sufficient power to promote that same chaotic view of reality which he was fighting against in his art; it is a paralysing kind of intuition. One of the specific abuses he mentions – the employment of children in factories (bk. VI, ch. 3,f) – is a case in point. In leaving reform to a change of heart promoted by a new leader who was to emerge from a monastery, Dostoevsky was surely abdicating his responsibilities.

Enough has been said on the subject of Dostoevsky's vitiated vision. And if these criticisms seem to imply a reproach to Dostoevsky for failing to uphold a practical ethic or to advocate specific reforms, a renewed attempt is needed to see the situation to which *The Brothers Karamazov* is addressed. It is particularly instructive to read the dis-

cussion of Dostoevsky by Thomas Masaryk.[7] This scholar and states-
man had unusually good qualifications for seeing Dostoevsky under
Western eyes: he had a deep knowledge and love of Russia; he was a
great believer in and practiser of liberal democracy; he was well read in
philosophy; he had good reason to uphold the Protestant ethic of
work; and he was heir to the revolutionary tradition of the Continent.
He was the perfect English critic without the insularity. Masaryk had
no difficulty in showing that Dostoevsky's solution was ineffectual,
since the monastic virtues he upheld were evolved in and could scarcely
exist outside an authoritarian society, so that they were unlikely to
lead to any very strong challenge to the *status quo*. Masaryk further
attacked him for treating nihilism as an essentially theological problem
and for failing to be an accurate historian (p. 150): ' he misjudges the
revolution and fails to analyse its motives, methods and scope.' But
what the point of this kind of historical judgment was Masaryk failed to
bring out, unless it was to show that revolution was not so very
hazardous a course after all: 'in all the states of Europe revolution had
actually mitigated and then eventually triumphed over absolutism.'
If Masaryk hoped that the dissemination of enlightened liberal ideas –
resting on a firmer understanding of social science than had been held
by the Russian liberals and radicals – could do something for Russia,
he was surely a victim of the liberal myth of history. Given the
political structure of Russia, sound liberal men were hardly likely to
have a lasting and determining voice; to suggest that they might was
less ridiculous, but only slightly so, than to put one's faith in Alesha's
community of boys. And to suppose that liberals could initiate a
revolution and hope to control it, now seems a dangerous delusion
(Masaryk had not seen the October Revolution). Because of the new
urban population, because of the rapid changes in the country following the abolition of serfdom, and because of the archaic autocracy and
the gulf between the intelligentsia and the people – Russia was ready for
a sweeping upheaval. Dostoevsky was mainly concerned with the
intelligentsia, yet this was hardly a limitation. The intelligentsia's
lack of a national tradition and their struggle to accommodate new
ideas were but another form and stage of the modernizing process
convulsing the whole Russian people. And in any event, disaffected
intellectuals in search of a role were natural revolutionary and political
leaders. In his understanding of his society and of the role of myth,
Dostoevsky was an anthropologist rather than a historian, and because

of this he was a better historian than Masaryk; he had a better understanding of what the nature of the revolution would be. Conrad, a man with qualifications similar to Masaryk's, had in addition the insight of literary genius, which enabled him to overcome his initial handicap – a dislike for Russia and for Dostoevsky – and to achieve in *Under Western Eyes* an insight comparable to Dostoevsky's own into the tragic situation of Russia, where action was the special province of brutes or where it conjured up forces mocking man's belief in his power to shape his world.

The dilemma of the Russian intelligentsia portrayed by Dostoevsky was his own personal dilemma. He could not have a European consciousness in a country which was not European; and yet what did it mean to be Russian when the traditional national consciousness had been shattered? It was his achievement in *The Idiot* and *The Devils* (and in *Crime and Punishment*) to find a form which dramatized this dilemma and revealed its nature. But the contingencies of his particular time and place in history limit his understanding when he turns to more general philosophical questions in *The Brothers Karamazov*. Perhaps this was an impossible novel to write. It lies somewhere between literature and eschatology. The solutions propounded by Dostoevsky (and by other prophetic writers) are more likely to lead to a cult than to a Church; and if a cult is not what we want, the danger is that a paralysing scepticism is all that is left to us. Dostoevsky can show that we shall be happier if we assume a basic harmony of the universe; he cannot show that this assumption is right.

The Brothers Karamazov matters not for its assertions and not for its denials but for its questions, to which there are no easy answers. A particularly famous one is Ivan's: will any world-order ever be justified if it requires the suffering of even one child? We can attempt to help those who are unhappy, as Dimitry dreams of doing in Siberia. We can try to protect children from future unhappiness as Alesha wishes to do. We can see that failure to act may be tantamount to causing yet more suffering. Yet the question has a force of its own which no answer can dissolve. It is left to nag us when Alesha asks if Christ is not entitled by his crucifixion to forgive even men who torture children. Avoiding a direct answer Ivan tells the legend of the Grand Inquisitor. Its implication is that Christ is as guilty as any man because of the suffering Christianity has brought to mankind, and further that Christ, the God-man, does not exist. Perhaps we should cease looking for explanations and accept that we shall be happier if we assume that evil and suffering are ultimately justified, and that we should simply do our part to enable others to share in the feast of life. The very form of this suggestion, however, appeals to a pragmatic consideration Dostoevsky would have rejected.

What then is there to be said about *The Brothers Karamazov*? Does Dostoevsky have no solution or fundamental outlook at all, as Bakhtin suggested? (perhaps this was a way of making Dostoevsky safe for study in Russia under Stalin). Or does Dostoevsky force us to recognize that there can be no solution and that we have to live our lives in a world of existential uncertainty? To say this is, despite the disclaimer, to impose a message on the novel. Surely these moves are misguided. Dostoevsky is important because of the questions he asks about his society and about the beliefs held by men in it, and above all because of his ability to dramatize the questions and show that they are real ones. They are close in substance and even in detail to the questions that still can and need to be asked almost everywhere as we are finally overtaken by the technological age. Dostoevsky's vision is distorted by the very problem to which he addresses himself, but this is a difficulty few radical social critics escape: how to find a standpoint from which to reject or transform society, even though we can hardly be free from the assumptions which shape it. In Dickens's novels institutions are never so completely stifling and ossified, nor individuals' sense of purpose so utterly lost, that there can be no hope. The chief hope in Dostoevsky's world is for a miracle. And if our situation is such that Dostoevsky's relevance eclipses Dickens's, it may be that our only ways out lie in prayer or in violence.

Notes

1   *The Brothers Karamazov*, bk. V, ch. 4; bk. VI, chs. 2 and 3.
2   Contrasts with the prison-world in *Little Dorrit* readily come to mind.
3   Bk. II, ch. 5; bk. III, ch. 7.
4   Bk. XI, ch. 9.
5   And if Bakhtin's characterization of Dostoevsky's novels as 'polyphonic' (in *Problemy tvorchestva Dostoevskogo*, Leningrad, 1929), a word which has been creeping into English criticism, means anything more than *dramatic*, I can understand it to be only that *up to a point*, compared with other writers, there is a greater difference in the frameworks of assumptions and questions we bring to bear on the various characters.

6 See bk. II, ch. 5.
7 *The Spirit of Russia*, vol. 3, ed. G. Gibian (New York, 1967). The material comprised in this volume was written after the 1905 revolution but before 1917, and was only recently found.

Conclusion:
Dickens's 'ideal' types

A favourite belief of Dostoevsky's was that his countrymen had a special gift for grasping the character and genius of other nations (sometimes he suspected that this was what being a Russian principally entailed). In the *Diary of a Writer* (1873)[1] he said by way of illustration: 'we understand Dickens in Russia, I am convinced, almost as well as the English, and maybe even all the subtleties; maybe even we love him no less than his own countrymen; and yet how typical, distinctive [*svoebrazen*], and national Dickens is.' This was a dangerous claim to make; when we read an author in translation – and we must remember that Dostoevsky read Dickens in Russian and French – it is easy to look for the 'main ideas' and to overlook inadequate realization. Dostoevsky's own affection for Little Nell suggests he was not immune to this tendency. The fact remains that his response to Dickens was a broad one. Humble men such as Tim Linkinwater and Tom Pinch are influences on, at any rate, some of the poor folk in Dostoevsky's early writings. The strongly drawn characters or 'caricatures' of Mrs Skewton reappear in *The Uncle's Dream*, and of Gashford and Chester in *The Devils*. Several of the more interesting studies attempted by Dickens – Edith Dombey, Mr Dorrit, Mr Micawber, and Steerforth – are put to good use by the Russian novelist. Pickwick is seen by him as a portrayal of the ideal. And there are sources which we have not considered here – the Marmeladovs are poor cousins of the Micawbers, while Creakle's cruelty towards young Copperfield leads to Arkady's sufferings at the hands of the schoolmaster Touchard in *The Raw Youth*.[2] All in all many conspicuous Dickensian types are counted among the influences: good rich men and humble little men, virtuous or angelic child figures, Byronic heroes, neurotics, villains, and buffoons.

If for a moment we confine ourselves to questions of method, they account for much of the differences between the originals and their Dostoevskian counterparts. Like the figures in Hogarth's dramatic cartoons or series, Dickens's characters are caught briefly in some action, the significance of which is conveyed by their attitudes, their gestures, and the setting as a whole. Two important elements in Dickens's art are his visual imagination and his use of stage techniques to express feelings and relationships. Of course the characters have voices as well – in the voices lies a major part of Dickens's genius – although the dialogue chiefly serves to define the characters and their attitudes rather than to prepare and advance the action. When a character can be presented mainly through speech and gesture, the English writer is unrivalled; Dostoevsky did not really know how to use Mrs Skewton in *The Uncle's Dream* (but Peter Verkhovensky is almost as compelling a ham-actor as Gashford or Chester). Dickens's visual gifts are strikingly displayed with Edith Dombey in those scenes which seem projections of her self-lacerating mind. His theatrical talents, on the other hand, are particularly apparent in Mr Dorrit. The lack of a genuine dramatic gift appears in that with his characters he is liable to resort to melodrama: sometimes from the moment they begin to act (Edith); at others, in the course of their interactions with other people (Little Dorrit's view of her father). Steerforth has considerable dramatic potential because of his author's loving puzzlement at him, but a sustained examination of feelings, motives, and behaviour is not Dickens's forte, and Steerforth turns into yet another melodramatic hero. These figures – Edith, Steerforth, and Dorrit – tax the resources of Dickens's art. They have a psychological interest which he cannot fully bring out; they are among his more interesting creations rather than his more successful ones. Consciously or not, Dostoevsky makes them into fully dramatic characters, so that they exist in a constantly changing relationship with each other and have a constantly redefined view or idea of themselves and of the world. He understands their psyche.

What is the importance of the influence? To say that Dostoevsky's characters are dramatic in a way their originals are not is not necessarily to say that he is the better writer. The flexibility and richness of Dickens's writing is lost when it is refracted through a Dostoevskian prism. In a general view of his art it would be necessary to consider how in some novels (above all *Great Expectations*) his visual and theatrical gifts, together with his feeling for the life and strangeness of language, combine to form whole structures in which the balance and tension between the parts yields as searching a view of society and man as we can find anywhere in the art of the novel. The overall power of Dickens's imaginative structures can carry those local weaknesses of realization which occur when he fails to fully understand or place a character (as with Mr Dorrit). The originality of the characters needs to be stressed (this goes with his ability to see the unusual and distinctive in ordinary men), as does the way he learns to turn his limitations as a dramatic writer into a distinct advantage. We can ask too whether with his theatrical characters he does not give a truer picture of the mass of mankind, and of what makes men's lives valuable, than do Dostoevsky or George Eliot with their highly conscious, dramatic characters; and we must bear in mind the limitations of 'dramatic' as a critical term, for it classes Dostoevsky's characters with George Eliot's and Tolstoy's, although his have so much greater an abnormality of psychology and situation. In the end technique is interesting in as much as it relates to subject. We cannot say that differences of method simply are differences of vision any more than that the differences of vision simply reflect differences between England and Russia in the nineteenth century. We can say that Dostoevsky's sense of drama could fully develop only in a country tortured by uncertainty over its role in history, just as Dickens's distinctive genius could lead to the great novels of his later period only because in his society there were continuing, relatively focused discussions about reforms, the meaning of work, and the distinctions between ranks.

The important discriminations we make between our two authors concern their visions of man and society. Here the problem of influence becomes particularly interesting as regards the actual shape taken by Dostoevsky's works and the way we understand them. Without Edith Dombey and Steerforth, would Nastasia and Stavrogin exist in the form we know them? Above all could they play the key roles they do? Nastasia's function is partly allegorical for besides being a masochist she is a figure embodying the crisis of Russia, and as for Stavrogin he is engaged, together with the group surrounding him, in a search for a new unifying myth. The record of Dostoevsky's work on the novels suggests that the meaning of Nastasia and Stavrogin was not yielded to him all at once; their symbolical nature is a result of the kinds of characters they are, rather than the other way round. Concern with the significance of characters was closely linked with the process of creating them. Nastasia was bound to appeal in some way to Myshkin's compassion, but without Edith Dombey's self-hatred she would hardly express the dilemma of a country forcefully exposed to an alien culture. Without Steerforth's strange exemption from ordinary standpoints of judgment, Stavrogin might not be the great creator and destroyer he is. Dostoevsky must have known how unusual characters like these were: in the opening of the last part of *The Idiot* he suggested (perhaps half-seriously) that there was such a thing as a literary type of the ordinary man, which was representative of the vast majority of mankind. In attempting to bring his unusual characters into significant relation with society and with a Christian norm, he was, I suspect, led to look for some wider significance in their strange, intractable natures.

Dostoevsky appreciated the power of Dickens's artistic vision (though there were parts of it he could not use and perhaps could not really see – a character such as Daniel Doyce, the fine comedy in the meeting of the Dorrits and the Merdles at Martigny, the sense that worthwhile qualities were involved in being a gentleman). We recall that he spoke of Dickens as a 'great Christian' and admired his humble characters. Apart from Tom Pinch, other candidates we can include in this category are Little Dorrit, Little Nell, and Clennam – a possible minor influence in *The Idiot*. It seems that Dostoevsky's admiration for these people was based not only on their humility but on the ideal of brotherhood and community associated with them. Concern for the regeneration of man and of society lay at the heart of his response to Dickens. If we are to talk of his hostility to society or of his response to Dickens's rebels, we should do so in relation to this aim they both shared; at the same time, we should remember that brotherhood led in the one to a fuller appreciation (a far from complacent one) of Victorian society, and in the other to ever more urgent attempts to find some answer to the threat of disintegration. The principal characters that influenced Dostoevsky can be seen in direct relationship to the problem of community or conversion. Pickwick was at the centre of a union of childlike beings; Edith was a victim of society turned rebel and forever excluded from the community of man; Steerforth might ride rough-shod over the feelings of the humble yet held out the promise of a new and freer existence; Mr Dorrit relied on the good will and charity of men while scarcely acknowledging the virtues on which he so utterly depended. For someone with Dostoevsky's sort of interest in society, their importance is plain. Given the nature of the evidence, any attempt to decide whether his basic response was sparked by the characters and the theatrical techniques used to render them, or by their part in Dickens's quest for a regenerated society, is bound to be artificial and misconceived. For Dostoevsky questions of form, theme, and vision were inseparable, as we shall see. The reasons why this was so are related, it will further appear, to the reasons why his critical comments refer to Dickens's good characters and never to his rebels.

In 'Apropros of the Exhibition'[3] Dostoevsky singles out several paintings for discussion – hunters telling tall stories by Perov, merchants listening to a nightingale by Makovsky, boat-haulers by Repin. Despite his praise for these pictures, he has one large reservation:

> Our genre has yet to rise to the level of Gogol and Dickens. . . .
> it lacks something that would enable it to move out or expand.
> For Dickens is genre, nothing more; but Dickens created
> 'Pickwick', 'Oliver Twist', and the 'Granddaughter and
> Grandfather' from the novel 'The Old Curiosity Shop'. No, our
> genre is still far from this; it still rests on 'Hunters and
> Nightingales'. Dickens has a multitude of Hunters and Nightingales
> but only in secondary places.

In *The Raw Youth* Dostoevsky himself 'paints' a genre-picture inspired by Dickens, when Trishatov, who has been wasting his life in company with disreputable friends suddenly confides in Arkady:[4]

> 'Say, Dolgoruky, have you read Dickens's *Old Curiosity Shop*?'
> 'I have. Why?'
> 'Do you remember – wait I'll drink another glass – do you
> remember one place at the end when they – the mad old man and
> the charming thirteen-year-old girl, his granddaughter, have at
> last after their fantastic flight and wanderings taken refuge near
> some medieval Gothic cathedral and the girl is given some sort of
> task there and shows the cathedral to visitors. – And one day
> the sun is setting, and this child is on the cathedral porch,
> with the last rays pouring over her, and she stands looking at
> the sunset with quiet thoughtful contemplation in her childlike
> soul, her soul astonished as if before some kind of riddle, for
> the one and the other are like a riddle – the sun like the thought
> of God and the cathedral like the thought of man – isn't that so?

Oh, I can't express it, but God loves the first such thoughts in children. – And there, on the stairs, next to her, that mad old man, the grandfather, is looking at her with an arrested gaze. – You know, there's nothing in it, nothing at all, in this picture of Dickens's, yet you will never forget it and it has remained for all Europe. – Why? Here is beauty! Innocence! Oh, I don't know what, but it is good. At school I was always reading novels. You know, I've got a sister in the country, only a year older than me! She and I were sitting on the terrace, under our old lime trees, and the sun was also setting, and suddenly we stopped reading and said to each other that we too would be kind, we would be beautiful – I was preparing for university and – Oh, Dolgoruky, you know we all have our memories.' (pt. III, ch. 5, iii)

This picture 'after Dickens' suffers from some of the vague generality characteristic of *The Old Curiosity Shop*. For one thing there is (as Futrell pointed out) no episode quite corresponding to this in the novel (although there is a scene where Nell and her grandfather rest beside a church as the sun is setting). For another, through the effect of translation or imagination, the church where the pair at last find refuge has been transformed into a cathedral (the monastery ruins mentioned by Dickens perhaps justify this). None the less the scene with its dreamlike Gothic setting is faithful to the spirit of Little Nell. Here, as so often in Dostoevsky's novels, the ideal is embodied in a pictorial image. The same spirit inspired several other iconographic representations – particularly the death scenes in *The Insulted and Injured* (Nellie), *The Eternal Husband* (Liza), and *Crime and Punishment* (the girl in Svidrigailov's dream). Little Nell is enshrined in Dostoevsky's work in the same way as the vision of the Golden Age he found in a painting by Claude Lorrain.

In his comments on genre Dostoevsky did not mean to set up a division between the arts, nor to suggest that Dickens's example was relevant only to painters or for the making of pictures in words (of course he would have acknowledged certain tasks were better suited to some art forms than to others). He himself turned Little Nell into a dramatic character in *The Insulted and Injured*, and he thought that Gogol as well as Dickens set a standard for Russian painters. Genre was concerned with the same portion of reality Dostoevsky had marked out for himself ('Apropos of the Exhibition'):[5]

Genre is the art of depicting contemporary, current reality [*deistvitel' nost'*], which the artist has felt for himself and seen with his own eyes, as opposed to, say, historical reality, which one cannot see with one's own eyes, and which is depicted not in its current form but in its completed form. (A *Nota bene*: we speak of 'seeing with one's own eyes.') Yet Dickens never saw Pickwick with his own eyes, but noted him in the diversity of the reality he observed; he created a person and presented him as the product of his observations. Thus this person is just as real as one truly existing, although Dickens took only an ideal of actuality [*ideal deistvitel'nosti*].

This notion of taking an 'ideal of actuality' contains one clue to what made Dickens's novels of particular interest for Dostoevsky in his own work, and to what set them apart from the mass of Gothic and melodramatic fiction. The comments on genre contain further hints:[6]

I even think that from the standpoint of genre, at the present moment in our art, so far as I can tell from certain signs, 'Pickwick' and the 'Granddaughter' would be seen as somehow [too] ideal; and our principal artists – as I have observed in conversation with some of them – fear the ideal as if an unclean force. No doubt an honourable fear, but an unjust, unfair prejudice. Our artists need more boldness, more independence of thought, and maybe more education. That, I think, is why our historical school, which seems to be lying still, is ailing. Apparently our modern artists are even afraid of historical painting and have given themselves up to genre, as the one true and legitimate channel for all talents. It seems to me as though an artist feels that he will have to 'idealize' in historical painting and, so, will have to lie. 'One must depict reality as it is', they say, when there is no such reality, and never has been on earth. For the essence of things is inaccessible to man, and he apprehends nature as it is reflected in his idea, after passing through his feelings [*chuvstva*]. Hence, he must give more freedom to the idea, and not fear the ideal.

Art had to illuminate reality, not mirror it.[7] The search for surface reality was liable to lead the artist into error. Dostoevsky, in some remarks aimed at Leskov, spoke of writers who chose some special field for themselves – for instance, merchants or peasants – and then went about, notebook in hand, listening for characteristic phrases to jot down. They would end up with several hundred phrases, and begin a novel; as soon as a merchant or a member of the clergy had to appear, a speech would be got up for him from the notes. But, protested Dostoevsky, all of this was a lie, for the characters were made to speak 'in essences', that is to say, as no one ever spoke in real life.[8] An artist looking for surface realism was particularly likely to be untrue to psychological reality and to artistic truth. In one of Leskov's stories ('The Sealed Angel'), a group of Old Believers returned to the fold of Orthodoxy after seeing a miracle happen; they were supposedly so impressed by the priest's love and kindness that they remained in the Church even after it turned out the miracle was a mere accident. Dostoevsky argued with rich sarcasm that no Old Believer would be converted to a church whose priest, as depicted by Leskov, had no more notion of holiness than a bureaucrat, and he further insinuated that the sham miracle betrayed an insecurity in Leskov's own beliefs.[9] A man's limitations and prejudices were bound to appear in his artistic work.

In calling for the artist to give 'more freedom to the idea' Dostoevsky was not suggesting that the interest of the work lay in the artist's own opinions. He claimed that the moment Griboedov stopped being an artist and started speaking for himself in *Woe From Wit* he lowered himself to a 'very unenviable level, incomparably lower even than the level of the representatives of our intelligentsia at that time'.[10] Not surprisingly, Dostoevsky warned in particular against the effects of a prior liberal commitment: 'Any work of art, without a preconceived tendency, executed only out of artistic necessity, and even on a quite unrelated subject having no hint of tendentiousness – will be far more useful for these same tendentious aims than, for instance, all the songs of a shirt (by our own writers, not Hood's), even though it appears to be what is called satisfaction of idle curiosity.'[11] He says that before seeing Repin's boat-haulers at the Exhibition of Russian Art he had been worried as the subject was such an obvious one for a social message. In the event his fears were groundless: 'It is impossible to imagine that a thought about the politico-economic and social duties of the upper classes to the people could have ever penetrated into the poor, worn head of this peasant beaten down by ever-lasting grief – and do you know, sweet critic, the humble innocence of thought of this peasant serves its purpose far better than you think – precisely your tendentious liberal purpose.'

An artist had to be open to experience and attempt to unite it in a view or idea; but he had to beware of the merely accidental as well as of preconceived ideas. 'The task of art is not the accidents of everyday life [*byt*] but their *general idea* [my italics], perspicuously guessed and faithfully taken from all the multiplicity of homogeneous phenomena of life.' [12] The medium through which this was to be done was character or type. 'All the depth, all the content of an artistic work is contained . . . only in its types or characters.' [13] An artist had a particular duty to see new types emerging and to find the direction society was taking. This could not be done by keeping to the paths marked out by previous writers: [14]

> Our artists (like any ordinary beings) first distinctly notice the manifestations of reality, consider their characteristic nature [*kharakternost'*], and work out the given type in art, only when the type is passing away and disappearing, and degenerating into another type, corresponding with the movement and development of the age; so that the almost old is always being served to us as something new. They themselves believe it is new, and not passing away. . . . Only a writer of genius or of very strong talent guesses the type *at the time* and presents it *in its time*.

What people called realism was often the familiar and hackneyed, and therefore they were inclined to question the truthfulness of an artist concerned with 'current reality'. In an oft-quoted letter to Strakhov, Dostoevsky wrote: [15]

> I have my own special view of reality (in art), and what the majority call almost fantastic and exceptional is for me sometimes the very essence of the real. The everydayness of phenomena and the established [*kazennyi*] view of them is still not realism in my opinion; in fact – rather the reverse. In every copy of the newspapers you can meet an account of the most real – and strange – facts. For our authors they are fantastic. . . . Who will note them, explain them, write them down? They occur continually and every day, and not exceptionally.

Dostoevsky went on to say in the same letter that his fantastic Idiot was no unreality, and that characters such as he must exist in the layers of Russian society that were detached from the land, layers that were themselves becoming increasingly fantastic. His wish to stress the realism of his method led him into making some confused suggestions. While he did publish several accounts of criminal cases, and used newspaper stories in his novels, his creative work could hardly be described as 'noting facts'. As his notebooks show, his own process of 'noting a character in the diversity of reality' – his description of Dickens's procedure for Pickwick – was an immensely complicated one. His problem with Prince Myshkin was to define the ideal of the perfectly beautiful man and to show what it might look like in modern Russian society. The question of whether Myshkin (or the other characters) did exist is largely a specious one, although it is true that they can be imagined as existing. What makes his characters *real* and *typical* is not so much their actual existence as what they have to tell us about the conflicts in Russian society, the way Russian society was going, the possibilities for good and evil in it, and the spiritual life of Russians in his day.

The creation of types was a task for all artists. What was peculiar to the novelist was a concern with the complexity of life.[16] 'The form of the novel was created because of the need for poetic idealization (typification) of the complexity of life.' Within the novel the 'poetic' figures had to interact with the secondary characters. Dostoevsky held that Russian novelists were less successful in this part of their task ('our poets are least of all novelists, and our novelists are first of all poets, and then novelists'). Thus he claimed that Leskov did succeed in creating some types in *Cathedral Folk* but that he 'wanted to be not only a poet but a novelist. He understands very well that a suitable setting and suitable changes of fortune should not only provide a beautiful framework for his heroes but should illuminate them well and be illuminated by them. The writer wanted to be a novelist, but here he is no longer an artist, a master.' Dostoevsky admired Dickens's 'ideal' or poetic characters even though his own heroes suffered from far more self-doubt and inner division. And if he felt that Dickens had not succeeded in the properly novelistic part of his task he never said so.

When Dostoevsky spoke of Pickwick as an 'ideal of actuality' he meant first of all that Dickens had found a 'general idea' related to his experience and embodied it in a 'type'. But Dostoevsky was almost certainly thinking of Pickwick as 'ideal' in a more than Hegelian sense. Running through his criticism there was a concern with positive types – with 'ideal' types in the sense of something to be aimed at. It was important to find not only what was happening to society but what hope there was for its regeneration. For instance the great achievement of *Cathedral Folk* was to do precisely this.

> The author is bringing figures from the Russian clergy into the field of our poetry for the first time . . . he is setting before us positive types from this milieu. In this way [he] is opening up for our poetry a new, as yet untouched part of the life of Russian society and the [Russian] people. This is a service of no little importance in itself, and of even greater importance in view of the critical position of our society. Again, as always, on thousands upon thousands of occasions, our poetry is moving ahead of society and reminding us of our strength amidst our impotence! (Vinogradov, p. 515)

The reasons that made Pickwick an 'ideal of actuality' are, it would likewise appear, closely connected with Dostoevsky's concern for the state of society.

Why was Dickens's work important to Dostoevsky? Dickens wanted to reform society. He sought to understand the whole of reality and to provide a perspective on it. His rich diversity of types was the necessary complement of this undertkaing. He was a great creator of 'typical, distinctive, and national' characters. Dostoevsky's own search for types was an essential part of his attempt to understand Russia; hence it is not surprising that many of the characters influenced by Dickens were presented as distinctively Russian. Both authors were subversives whose radicalism was based neither on faith in institutions nor on revolution. Because they wished to change society, they were particularly aware of all who were opposed to it. Dickens was a 'national' writer in a way few contemporary Russians managed to be, for either they were describing the old congealed forms of society, instead of the new emerging ones, or they tended to identify with the liberal or radical denigration of their country, or they were too uncommitted to anything. Dostoevsky levelled one or another of these complaints against such writers as Tolstoy, Turgenev, Leskov, and Shchedrin, even though in his hands the search for a way of renewing society chiefly served to uncover its shaky foundations. Tortured national pride may underlie his boast that 'every European poet, thinker, philanthropist, is always – in the whole world apart from his own country – best and most inwardly understood and accepted in Russia. Shakespeare, Byron, Walter Scott, Dickens – are more akin and understandable to the Russians, than, for instance, to the Germans, although of course the copies of their works going about in translations here are not a tenth of the number in book-full Germany.' But another assertion he made in the same place[17] holds good in its application to his own use of Dickens: 'Every European poet or innovator, everybody who goes through over there with a new thought and a new force, cannot fail to become at once a Russian poet as well, cannot fail to change Russian thought, and become an almost Russian force.'

Notes

1 'Apropos of the Exhibition.'
2 See Futrell, 'Dostoyevsky and Dickens', *English Miscellany*, ed. Mario Praz, 7 (1956).
3 *Diary of a Writer* (1873). *Dnevnik pisatelia* (Paris, 1951), vol. 1, pp. 483f.
4 *Sobranie sochinenii*, vol. 8, pp. 483f.
5 *Dnevnik pisatelia*, vol. 1, p. 282.
6 *Ibid.*, vol. 2, p. 281.
7 See R. L. Jackson, *Dostoevsky's Quest for Form.*
8 'Disguised' ('Riazhennyi'), *Diary of a Writer* (1873). *Dnevnik pisatelia* (Paris, 1951), vol. 1, p. 298.
9 'Marred Appearance' ('Smiatennyi vid'), *Diary of a Writer* (1873). *Ibid.*, pp. 251–5.
10 *Diary of a Writer* (1876), April, ch. 1, ii. *Ibid.*, vol. 2, p. 150.
11 'Apropos of the Exhibition'. *Ibid.*, vol. 1, p. 277.
12 'Disguised.' *Ibid.*, p. 290.
13 *Diary of a Writer* (1876), April, ch. 1, ii. *Ibid.*, vol. 2, p. 150.
14 'Disguised.' *Ibid.*, vol. 1, p. 299.
15 No. 323, *Pis'ma*, vol. 2.
16 The following quotations come from a review of *Cathedral Folk* which V. V. Vinogradov has identified as Dostoevsky's (*Problema avtorstva i teoriia stilei*, Moscow, 1961, pp. 515f.). Similar statements could be supplied from *Diary of a Writer*.
17 'George Sand's Death', *Diary of a Writer* (1876). *Dnevnik pisatelia*, vol. 2, pp. 230f.

Select bibliography

Amerongen, J. B. van, *The Actor in Dickens: A Study of the Histrionic and Dramatic Elements*, London, 1926.

Arban, Dominique, *Dostoievski: 'Le Coupable'*, Paris, 1953.

Auden, W. H., 'Dingley Dell and the Fleet', *The Dyer's Hand*, New York, 1962.

Averkiev, D. V., 'Kratkii ocherk zhizni i pisatel'stva F. M. Dostoevskogo', in Dostoevsky, *Polnoe sobranie sochinenii*, 6 vols (St Petersburg, 1886), vol. 1.

Bakhtin, M. M., *Problemy tovorchestva Dostoevskogo*, Leningrad, 1929; rev. edn., Moscow, 1963.

Balzac, Honoré de, *Evgeniia Grande* [*Eugénie Grandet*], trans. F. M. Dostoevsky, ed. L. P. Grossman, Moscow-Leningrad, 1935.

Belinsky, V. G., *Polnoe sobranie sochinenii*, 13 vols, Moscow, 1953–9.

Bel'chikov, N. F., *Dostoevsky v protsesse petrashevtsev*, Moscow-Leningrad, 1936.

Bem, A. L., 'Evoliutsiia obraza Stavrogina: K sporu ob "Ispovedi Stavrogina" ' (unpublished paper deposited in the British Museum).

——, *Faust v tvorchestve Dostoevskogo*, Zapiski nauchno-issledovatel'skogo ob'edineniia, 5(x), Section des sciences philosophiques, historiques et sociales, no. 29, Prague, 1937.

——, 'Giugo [Hugo] i Dostoevsky', *Slavia*, 15 (1937–8), 73–86.

——, 'Pervye shagi Dostoyevskogo (genesis romana *Bednye lyudi*)' , *Slavia*, 12 (1933–4), 134–61.

——, ed., *O. Dostoevskom*, 3 vols, Prague, 1929, 1933, 1936.

Berkov, P., 'Dikkens v Rossii', *Literaturnaia entsiklopediia*, vol. 3, Moscow, 1930.

Butt, John, & Tillotson, Kathleen, *Dickens at Work*, London, 1957.

Chesterton, G. K., *Charles Dickens*, London, 1906.

Collins, Philip, *Dickens and Crime*, 2nd edn, London, 1964.

Dabney, R. H., *Love and Property in the Novels of Dickens*, London, 1967.

Dickens, Charles, *New Oxford Illustrated Dickens*, 21 vols, 1947–58.

——, *The Speeches of Charles Dickens*, ed. Fielding, London, 1960.

——, in Russian (the complete list of translations available to Dostoevsky is much longer):
Barnaby Rudge, in *Otechestvennye zapiski* (1842)
David Copperfield, trans. Vvedensky in *Otechestvennye zapiski* (1851)

Dombey and Son, trans. Vvedensky in *Sovremennik* (1847–8) and in *Otechest-vennye zapiski* (1847–8)
Little Dorrit, in *Otechestvennye zapiski* (1856–7)
Martin Chuzzlewit, in *Otechestvennye zapiski* (1844)
Nicholas Nickleby, in *Biblioteka dlia chteniia* (1840)
Pickwick Papers, in *Biblioteka dlia chteniia* (1840), and trans. Vvedensky in *Otechestvennye zapiski* (1849–50)

Dolinin, A. S., 'Dostoevsky sredi petrashevtsev', *Zven'ia*, ed. Vlad. Bonch-Burevich, 6 (1936), 512–45.

——, ed., *F. M. Dostoevsky- Materialy i issledovaniia*, Leningrad, 1936.

——, ed., *F. M. Dostoevsky: Stat'i i materialy*, 2 vols, Petrograd, 1922; Moscow-Leningrad, 1925

——, *F. M. Dostoevsky v vospominaniiakh sovremennikov*, 2 vols, Moscow, 1964.

Dostoevskaia, Anna G., *Dnevnik 1867 g.*, Moscow, 1923.

——, *Vospominaniia*, ed. L. P. Grossman, Moscow-Leningrad, 1925.

Dostoevsky, Aimée [Dostoevskaia, Liubov'], *Fyodor Dostoyevsky: A Study*, London, 1921.

Dostoevsky, F. M., *Dnevnik pisatelia*, 3 vols, Paris, YMCA Press [1951].

——, 'F. M. Dostoevsky v rabote nad romanom Prodrostok: Tvorcheskie rukopisi', *Literaturnoe nasledstvo*, vol. 77, Moscow, 1965.

——, *Iz arkhiva F. M. Dostoevskogo: Idiot, Neizdannye materialy*, ed. P. N. Sakulin and N. F. Bel'chikov, Moscow-Leningrad, 1931.

——, *Pis'ma*, ed. A. S. Dolinin, 4 vols, Moscow-Leningrad, 1928–59.

——, *Polnoe sobranie sochinenii*, vols 22 and 23, *Zabitye i neizvestnye stranitsy*, ed. L. P. Grossman, Petrograd, Prosveshchenie [1918] (supplements to *Polnoe sobranie sochinenii*, 21 vols, St Petersburg, Prosveshchenie [1911]).

——, *Sobranie sochinenii*, ed. L. P. Grossman et al., 10 vols, Moscow, 1956–8.

——, *Stat'i*, in *Polnoe sobranie khudozhestvennykh sochinenii*, ed. B. V. Toma-shevsky and K. I. Khalabaev, 13 vols (Moscow-Leningrad, 1926–30), vol. 13.

——, *Zapisnye tetradi F. M. Dostoevskogo*, ed. E. N. Konshina, Moscow-Leningrad, 1935.

Fanger, Donald, *Dostoevsky and Romantic Realism: A Study of Dostoevsky in Relation to Balzac, Dickens and Gogol*, Harvard Studies in Comparative Literature, no. 27, Cambridge, Mass., 1965.

——, ed., *O Dostoevskom: Stat'i*, Brown University Slavic Reprint, 4, 1966.

Ford, George H., *Dickens and his Readers: Aspects of Novel Criticism Since 1836*, Princeton, 1965.

——, & Lane, Lauriat, eds, *The Dickens Critics*, Ithaca, N.Y., 1961.

Forster, John, *The Life of Charles Dickens*, 3 vols, London, 1872–4.

Frank, Joseph, 'Dostoevsky and the Socialists', *Partisan Review*, 32 (1965), 409–22.

——, 'Nihilism and Notes from the Underground', *Sewanee Review*, 69 (1961), 1–33.

Frank, Joseph, 'The World of Raskolnikov', *Encounter*, 26 (June 1966), 30–40.

Futrell, Michael H., 'Dostoyevsky and Dickens', *English Miscellany*, ed. Mario Praz, 7 (1956), 41–89.

Garis, Robert, *The Dickens Theatre: A Reassessment of the Novels*, London, 1965.

Gissing, George, *Charles Dickens*, London, 1898.

Gross, John, & Pearson, Gabriel, *Dickens and the Twentieth Century*, London, 1962.

Grossman, Leonid P., *Bor'ba za stil'*, Moscow, 1923.

——, *Dostoevsky*, Moscow, 1965.

——, 'Dostoevsky i chartistskii roman', *Voprosy literatury*, 1 (April 1959), 147–58.

——, 'Gofman [Hoffmann], Balzak, i Dostoevsky', *Sofiia*, 5 (1914), 87–96.

——, *Tvorchestvo Dostoevskogo*, in *Sobranie sochinenii*, 5 vols, Moscow, 1928, vol. 2, pt. 2.

——, ed., *Seminarii po Dostoevskomu: Materialy, bibliografiia i kommentarii*, Moscow, 1922.

——, ed., *Tvorchestvo Dostoevskogo, 1821–1881–1921: Sbornik statei i materialov*, Odessa, 1921.

——, & Polonsky, Viach., *Spor o Bakunine i Dostoevskom*, Leningrad, 1926.

Howard, David, Lucas, John, & Goode, John, *Tradition and Tolerance in Nineteenth-Century Fiction*, London, 1966.

Ivanov, Viacheslav, *Freedom and the Tragic Life*, trans. Cameron, London, 1952.

Jackson, R. L., *Dostoevsky's Quest for Form: A Study of his Philosophy of Art*, New Haven, Conn., 1966.

Johnson, Edgar, *Charles Dickens: His Tragedy and Triumph*, 2 vols, New York, 1953.

Katarsky, I. M., *Dikkens v Rossii: Seredina XIX veka*, Moscow, 1966.

——, & Fridlender, Iu. V., *Charl'z Dikkens: Bibliografiia russkikh perevodov i kritischeskoi literatury na russkom iazyke, 1838–1960*, Moscow, 1962.

Katkov, G., 'Steerforth and Stavrogin: On the Sources of the Possessed', *Slavonic and East European Review*, 27 (1949), 469–88.

Kirpotin, V. Ia., *F. M. Dostoevsky: Tvorcheskii put' (1821–1859)*, Moscow, 1960.

——, *Dostoevsky, v shestidesiatye gody*, Moscow, 1966.

Komarovich, V., *Dostoevsky: Sovremennye problemy istoriko-literaturnogo izucheniia*, Leningrad, 1925.

Laing, R. D., *The Self and Others*, London, 1961.

Leavis, F. R., 'Dombey and Son', *Sewanee Review*, 70 (1962), 177–201.

——, *The Great Tradition*, London, 1948.

Lesser, Simon O., 'Saint and Sinner – Dostoevsky's Idiot', *Modern Fiction Studies*, 4 (1958), 211–24.

Lewes, George H., 'Dickens in Relation to Criticism', *Fortnightly Review*, 17 (1872), 141–54.

Select bibliography

Marcus, Steven, *Dickens: From Pickwick to Dombey*, London, 1965.

Masaryk, Thomas, *The Spirit of Russia*, vol. 3, ed. G. Gibian, New York, 1967.

Mochul'sky, K., *Dostoevsky: Zhizn' i tvorchestvo*, Paris, 1947.

Muchnic, Helen, 'Dostoevsky's English Reputation', in *Smith College Studies in Modern Language*, 20 (1939).

Nabokov, Vladimir, *Nikolai Gogol*, New York, 1961.

Orwell, George, *Critical Essays*, London 1946.

Passage, Charles, *Dostoevski the Adapter: A Study in Dostoevski's Use of the Tales of Hoffmann*, University of North Carolina Studies in Comparative Literature, vol. 10, Chapel Hill, 1954.

Praz, Mario, *The Hero in Eclipse in Victorian Literature*, London, 1956.

Reizov, B. G., 'K voprosu o vliianii Dikkensa na Dostoevskogo', *Iazyk i literatura*, 5 (1930), 253–70.

Seeley, F. F., 'Dostoevsky's Women', *Slavonic and East European Review*, 39 (1961), 291–312.

Shtakenshneider, E. A., *Dnevnik i zapiski*, Moscow-Leningrad, 1934.

Simmons, Ernest, *Dostoevsky: The Making of a Novelist*, London, 1950.

Steiner, George, *Tolstoy or Dostoevsky: An Essay in Contrast*, London, 1960.

Stepanov, N. L., *et al.*, eds, *Tvorchestvo F. M. Dostoevskogo*, Moscow, 1969.

Strakhov, N. N., *Biografiia, pis'ma i zametki iz zapisnoi knizhki F. M. Dostoevskogo*, St Petersburg, 1883.

Venturi, Franco, *Roots of Revolution: A History of the Populist and Socialist Movements in Nineteenth Century Russia*, trans. Francis Haskell, London, 1960.

Vinogradov, V. V., *Evoliutsiia russkogo naturalizma: Gogol' i Dostoevsky*, Leningrad, 1929.

——, *Problema avtorstva i teoriia stilei*, Moscow, 1961.

Vogüé, E. M. de, *Le Roman russe*, Paris, 1886.

Wellek, René, *Dostoevsky: A Collection of Critical Essays*, Twentieth Century Views, Englewood Cliffs, N.J., 1962.

Wexler, Alexandra, 'Dickens und Dostojewski', *Deutsche Rundschau*, 8 August 1962.

Wilson, Edmund, *The Wound and the Bow*, Cambridge, Mass., 1941.

Zamotin, I. I., *F. M. Dostoevsky, v russkoi kritike: Chast' pervaia, 1846–1881*, Warsaw, 1931.

Zander, L. A., *Taina dobra (Problema dobra v tvorchestve Dostoevskogo)*, Frankfurt, 1960.

Index

Index

I   NAMES AND AUTHORS

169

II DICKENS

(Italic numbers refer to the most important discussions.)

III DOSTOEVSKY

Index

IV DOSTOEVSKY AND DICKENS